Carmelo Anthony: The Inspiring Story of One of Basketball's Most Versatile Scorers

An Unauthorized Biography

By: Clayton Geoffreys

Table of Contents

Foreword

2003 is often lauded as the beginning of the latest generation of NBA greats due to the draft class accounting for some of the most incredibly talent to hit the league since Michael Jordan. Superstars such as LeBron James, Chris Bosh, and Dwayne Wade started their illustrious NBA careers that year. And among that crowd of NBA stars was Carmelo Anthony, selected third overall by the Denver Nuggets. Since joining the NBA, Carmelo Anthony has demonstrated why he is one the most versatile scorers in the entire NBA. Pick a spot on the court, and Melo can score from there. His relentless ability to put the ball in the basket has made him into one of the deadliest scorers in the game of basketball today. Thank you for purchasing *Carmelo Anthony: The Inspiring Story of One of Basketball's Most Versatile Scorers*. In this unauthorized biography, we will learn Carmelo Anthony's incredible life story and impact on the game of basketball. Hope you enjoy and if you do, please do not forget to leave a review!

Also, check out my website at claytongeoffreys.com to join my exclusive list where I let you know about my latest books. To thank you for your purchase, you can go to my site to download a free copy of *33 Life Lessons: Success Principles, Career*

Advice & Habits of Successful People. In the book, you'll learn from some of the greatest thought leaders of different industries on what it takes to become successful and how to live a great life.

Cheers,

Clayton Geoffreys

Visit me at www.claytongeoffreys.com

Introduction

"Nothing will work unless you do." These wise words were uttered by the young and immensely gifted Carmelo Anthony, who has not always been an outstanding player. He had the will, but he had to grow into the skill. He was crazy about basketball as a youngster, but the small forward had to work hard to perfect his game. Today, he is just beginning to fulfill his potential as a genuine leader and is carving out his legacy in the NBA.

Since his start as a standout high school player, Anthony has not been a stranger to tenacity and hard work, and he has evolved from a rough stone into a multi-faceted gem. Real basketball fanatics have both positive and negative things to say about Anthony and his impact on basketball. Some view him as a selfish ball-hog who spends too much time showboating. They may even go on to say Melo is too caught up with putting up numbers instead of trying to help his team win.

On the other hand, others hail him as a sensational scoring machine, desperate to earn a ring. He may even be the most complete scorer the game has seen in quite a while, and that accolade alone is enough to rack up some wins. When it comes to offensive arsenals, nobody else in the game has more weapons than Melo. He has a deadly jumper that he can hit even with hands right in front of him. With a quick first step, he blows by slower defenders. Anthony could arguably be the best small forward down at the low post. Despite those talents, Carmelo has always lacked the accolades.

Regardless of his motives, Anthony is shaping up as a diamond in the rough. Like a billboard in Times Square, all of his strengths and weaknesses have been put on display for all to see. After more than a decade in the league, he has developed a game that is not likely to see any significant overhauls between now and his retirement. Even so, as with any precious gem, he still needs to be polished.

Defensively, he can be dull and often lacking in effort. Critics are quick to accuse him of losing focus and not connecting enough with his teammates to execute defensive plays. The thing is that Carmelo does not drop the defensive ball when he is in one-on-one and face-to-face situations. When defending on the ball, Melo cold keep up with the best of them. No, his most glaring flaw is in main "offensive player movement" situations.

Surprisingly, other teams are penetrating with an average adjusted field goal rate of 56.3%. In pick-and-roll situations, his defensive points-per-possession is at a staggering 1.06, which is slightly disappointing coming from a 6'8", 230-lb frame. He has the athletic physique to become a skillful defensive player. Based on his size alone, nobody would doubt that he could be an active, lean, defense machine. While he has proven that he can handle defensive rebounding, it is expected that he should also be able to manage to keep the guys in front, pressuring the ball. Unfortunately, he has not done so because his focus has always been on the other side of the floor.

However, he shines brightly when it comes to the offense. Anthony's one-and-done college season, masterfully crafted with spectacular shooting and consistent scoring, climaxed in an NCAA championship for Syracuse. He was a tremendous offensive weapon even back in college, and it did not surprise many that he brought the same game to the NBA. There was no doubt in anyone's mind that he was the best college player that year. It was evident from his statistics and championship-winning freshman year.

When Carmelo Anthony took his wares to the NBA, he did not take a second to adjust to the style of the big boys. He was immediately an explosive scorer in his rookie season. Melo was the highest scorer among all rookies that season, and his scoring numbers even put to shame veteran players who had been in the league for about a decade. However, he did not win the Rookie of the Year award that season because of a teenager in Cleveland named LeBron James. Nevertheless, Anthony has developed into one of the league's deadliest and most complete scorers who can explode on any given day.

Among his many NBA achievements, Anthony can boast being named an All-Star in several different seasons and an All-NBA Team selection on multiple occasions and different teams. Basketball fans will not soon forget the Team USA Olympic record of 37 points that he set in 2012 against Nigeria. As a player for the Denver Nuggets, he has been the best player on a team that made the playoffs since 2004, his rookie season, up to 2010, his final full year with Denver. And after two decades of absence in the Conference Finals, Melo was able to bring his team to within arm's length of an NBA Finals appearance back in 2009. As a New York Knick, who can forget the record-breaking career-high of 62 points in the Garden against Charlotte during the 2013-2014 season? These milestones cannot be ignored. Anthony can pretty much score from anywhere on the court, but many wonder if he is a cornerstone on which one can build a team.

Despite his accolades and individual accomplishments, the most significant knock on Anthony's NBA career has always been the lack of overall team success and an NBA championship.

None of the teams he has been on has ever been in the NBA Finals, and Melo has only been in the Conference Finals once in his career. The lack of team success has also been a contributing factor to why Carmelo Anthony has never been an NBA Most Valuable Player. However, his lack of championships was never because he had a bad supporting cast surrounding him.

Melo had the luxury of playing alongside the likes of Allen Iverson, Chauncey Billups, and Amar'e Stoudemire, but he could never get over the hump. With teammates like JR Smith, Tyson Chandler, Nene, Marcus Camby, and Andre Miller supporting him, Carmelo's supporting cast was not bad either. He has even had future Hall of Fame coaches mentoring him. However, it was always a wonder why he could never get over the hump.

With his ability to score points in a hurry coupled with his lack of success as a winner, Carmelo Anthony was a polarizing figure in New York. He loved the Big Apple and playing as a Knick. However, the Knicks' regular player and staff changes and rebuilding periods never got Anthony much success in New York. Many would even say that he was the one thing that held Kristaps Porzingis back from being the new franchise player.

Believing his window of opportunity was closing and realizing that the New York Knicks were better off rebuilding with younger players, Melo and the Knicks parted ways during the 2017 offseason. Anthony was traded to the Oklahoma City Thunder to team up with fellow superstars Russell Westbrook and Paul George. The Thunder were hailed as the newest super team in the NBA when they acquired a player of Carmelo Anthony's stature.

With star teammates in Westbrook and George, Carmelo Anthony is now in a situation he has never been in before. Never has Melo played with two superstars. He is in an entirely new position, and some would not expect him to be the leader and go-to guy on the team. But with such a collection of talent surrounding him, anything but a deep playoff run would be a failure for both Melo and the Thunder. And if they would indeed fail, some would be quick to point fingers at Carmelo Anthony.

Nevertheless, Carmelo Anthony has long been one of the best players in the world and has been among the top small forwards in the NBA since his entry in 2003. He has had some of the best scoring nights in recent memory, and he is one of the most polarizing personalities in the NBA because of his equally polarizing scoring abilities. Nobody could question his talents, and his skills at the offensive end are undeniable. The only doubt is his ability to make everyone better. But with the burden now divided between him and his fellow star teammates, Melo may not even have to make others better. He would just have to be himself—a deadly scorer that could win games with just a stroke of his hand.

Chapter 1: Childhood and Early Life

To understand where Anthony is going, it is essential to know where he came from. Underneath the eroded surfaces of the drug-infested streets of Baltimore, Maryland, lay a precious stone waiting to be mined and polished.

Carmelo Kyam Anthony was born in the South Brooklyn neighborhood of Red Hook on May 29, 1984, of mixed heritage. His dad, Carmelo Sr., who died due to liver failure when Anthony was just a toddler, was Puerto Rican, while his mom, Mary, is African-American. The death of Carmelo Sr. left Mary to raise the family on her own. While some NBA superstars were abandoned by their fathers, Melo's dad would have undoubtedly remained to raise his children, but sadly could not stay with his family. The Anthony family moved to a Baltimore area known as "The Pharmacy" when he was just 8. Some may recognize this area as it was made famous on HBO's "The Wire," and it was just as dangerous when Carmelo and his mom lived there. In fact, crime was rampant on just about every street corner. Melo's childhood friend Kelly Minor once said that everything rough you could think about happens in that part of the city. However, he would also say that surviving under those conditions makes a man tougher.

It took time before the young Melo figured out what he wanted to do for life. Nevertheless, he was always competitive. He always wanted to pitch whenever he played baseball with the other kids. Carmelo Anthony was also an excellent wide receiver in football when he was young. Naturally, Anthony was as good of an athlete as anyone.[i]

However, Anthony's goal was basketball. He began playing basketball with his older brothers when he was 7, and it did not take him long to start carving out his reputation. He joined competitions and was recognized in many Youth League tournaments. Sports proved to be vital for his departure from the violence and drug dealing that were prevalent in his neighborhood. His mom wanted better for her youngest son, and she commanded the upper hand by leveraging basketball as a powerful tool to keep the young Anthony off the streets and out of trouble. If he stepped out of line even a little, he was not allowed to go near the basketball courts, which were like a second home for Anthony.

Basketball was the young Melo's escape from reality. He would stay up all day just to watch college or NBA basketball games. New York was always a hotbed when it comes to basketball, and many college programs at that time had great prospects playing for them. Growing up as a Knicks fan, Carmelo had the pleasure of being able to watch Patrick Ewing's glory days in New York wherein he dominated and led the team to an NBA Finals appearance. Carmelo Anthony was just crazy about the game of basketball and was a fan of it at every level. His obsession with the game could have contributed to how he blossomed into an excellent NBA player.

However, Carmelo Anthony was not a gifted basketball player in his younger years. In middle school, Melo's role on the team was ball boy. He was always there in the background unnoticed by even the coaches. He was not even good enough to get the attention of the coaching staff. But the young Anthony worked harder to get to where he is now.[i]

Never one to back down from a fight, Carmelo Anthony would watch fellow future NBA player Rasual Butler from afar in a basketball tournament. Butler was five years older than Melo, who was in seventh grade at that time. The more experienced player was a star in high school and received numerous individual and all-team selections. Nonetheless, Anthony challenged the older and better player to one-on-one games. Though Rasual's size and experience often got the best of Anthony, the younger player never backed down and hated losing. They would seem like equals out on the perimeter before

Butler would resort to dominating the smaller Anthony down low.[i]

Rasual Butler remembers that time all too well. It was lunchtime during that basketball tournament. While other players were nowhere to be found because they were having their meals, Carmelo Anthony was still out on the floor thinking that he had to get better. That was when he started challenging Butler. Though Rasual would admit that he was the better player because of his height, he already believed that Melo was already exceptional at that time.

Butler would never see Melo again after that encounter. The next time the two players met was when Carmelo Anthony was already in the NBA. Butler was shocked at how big and how good Anthony had become. The young forward was only looking up to Rasual several years back. But in the NBA, Carmelo was already miles ahead of Butler regarding skills. It was a funny reversal of roles for the two future NBA players.[i]

Chapter 2: High School Years

Though Anthony was nuts about basketball and spent considerable time on the courts, he was not much of a superstar at the beginning of his career. At that point, his size was very different from the strikingly tall man that we know today. Back then, he was not the tallest guy on the court. Even when he first played the game as a point guard, he was not a tall kid for that position.

Anthony entered Towson Catholic High School in 1998 but was not able to play at all that year. He was cut from the school's varsity team, and it left him broken. But another NBA player once had the same kind of experience. Michael Jordan was once cut from his high school team. That day made MJ more obsessed with becoming great. A decade later, he became the best basketball player in the history of the game. For Anthony's part, getting cut from the team only served as a motivation for him to become better as a player.

It was also that year when a short and developing Carmelo Anthony figured out what he wanted to do most and where he wanted to play. Watching the 1998 All-Star Game played at Madison Square Garden in New York, Melo saw a glimpse of the best basketball talents playing in the world's most famous arena. It was his first time watching the All-Star Game.[ii]

Carmelo Anthony's best memory at that time was when he saw Michael Jordan playing in his final midseason classic. On the other end, there was Kobe Bryant, who, at 19 years old, became the youngest All-Star in league history. Jordan guarded Bryant, and Kobe never backed down from Mike either. It was a symbolic passing of the guard from one all-time great to a future league legend.[ii]

Out on the stands, Carmelo Anthony was watching and taking pictures of the Greatest of All Time matching up with the Black Mamba. He had always revered MJ since he was young. Soon after, he would begin idolizing Kobe as well. After that experience, Anthony knew that he wanted to belong amongst those greats. As we are aware, not long after that, Carmelo Anthony would somehow find himself matched up with Bryant in the All-Star Game.

That was also when Melo started dreaming about playing for New York. When he was there watching, no Knick was representing New York in that game. Not even the great Patrick Ewing was playing. Because of that, and after seeing MJ playing in the MSG for the midseason classic in 1998, Anthony would dream about becoming a Knick and representing the city of New York in the All-Star Game someday.[ii]

Ten months and five inches later, the determined and inspired Melo rose to become one of Baltimore's best young basketball talents. He had worked hard on his ball-handling skills and jump shots as a guard. His exceptional ball-handling and shooting ability carried over into the body of a wingman who stood taller than most of his peers. Anthony was on his way to a future as a dangerously packed wingman who had the ball-handling ability of a point guard and the shooting ability of an off-guard.

He suddenly began to brand himself as one of the area's stellar players was even awarded as the Metro Player of the Year and the Baltimore Catholic League Player of the Year in 2001. In his second year in high school, he averaged 14 points, five rebounds, and four assists. With Anthony on the team, Towson Catholic was nearly unbeatable with a 26-3 record. However, they were merely third in the state tournament. It was a surprising turnaround for a kid who had been cut from the team a year ago but had now become one of its best players.

Anthony's junior year in high school was great. He almost doubled his numbers. His scoring increased to 23 points per game while he doubled his rebounds with 10.3 per outing. Whoever decided not to let Anthony onto the team two years past must have felt his jaw drop a few dozen times, as Melo was the best player on his high school team. Despite a successful year, it was not without incident. Distracted by the attention that he was receiving, Anthony was often truant and in trouble in school for missing days. While many began to think that the recognition and possibility of making it big were getting to his head, the scrawny and weak Anthony went virtually unnoticed by scouts.

Admittedly, the NBA would not likely be his next stop just yet, as he was not prepared for the physicality of the NBA game. He was still only a scrawny high school kid who could not match up well with bigger and stronger wingmen in the NBA. Incidentally, at this time, Towson Catholic came just within reach of the state title. Nevertheless, it was a terrific individual year for Carmelo Anthony as he was named Player of the Year in three different categories.

That set the wheels in motion. Despite just entering his senior year in high school, many colleges lined up for Carmelo Anthony's services. The most interested ones were Syracuse and North Carolina. When Anthony realized he was on Syracuse's watch list, he buckled down and began taking his studies more seriously. During that time, the prep-school-to-pro fad was prominent in the NBA. The NBA was seeing an influx of high school players like Kobe Bryant and Kevin Garnett. Those guys went on to have stellar NBA careers despite not having been able to go to college. As a high school player, Melo was already good enough to join the ranks of those players.

Anthony, however, made a bold move that went against the grain. Just before starting his senior year of high school, Anthony decided to declare early and announced that he would be attending Syracuse University after graduation. From a kid growing up in Brooklyn, Anthony had always followed Syracuse and the Orangemen. He was a fan of Coach Jim Boeheim's approach to the game and the progress of players under his leadership. Anthony saw Syracuse as an opportunity to get plenty of exposure and shine in the Big East Conference.

However, there was one problem: Melo was not doing well enough in school to make a Division I NCAA team. His ACT scores were subpar. To even be considered an academic prospect, he would have to work harder outside the realms of basketball and inside the confines of a study room. Anthony and his mother pondered the options, and they agreed that he could get better grades if he transferred to another school.

Carmelo Anthony's family considered going to Oak Hill Academy, a boarding school in Virginia that has never had a losing season in basketball. Talks with Head Coach Steve Smith removed any doubts and sealed the deal. The up-and-coming superstar transferred to Oak Hill Academy for his senior year. Meanwhile, Anthony led his Baltimore AAU team to the Final Four of the Adidas Big Time Tournament. Anthony stood out in the tournament, averaging 25.2 points per game, which caught the eye of NBA bigwigs. He also played at the USA Basketball Youth Development Festival where he helped the East Team win the silver medal. He even went on to play LeBron James toe-to-toe. The two future NBA superstars scored 24 points apiece and formed a friendship that lasts to date.

As a senior at Oak Hill, Anthony averaged 21.7 points and eight rebounds. He was named All-USA First-Team and a First-Team All-American. He went on to score 27 points in the Jordan Brand game. The 2002 McDonald's All-American Game foreshadowed Anthony's professional career. In that match, he teamed up with future teammates Amar'e Stoudemire and Raymond Felton. He scored 19 points in that exhibition game and played with and against many skilled high school players. Melo also went on to display his athletic abilities by winning the dunk contest. Anthony's standout performance among the top secondary school prospects caused him to be named as one of the top, if not the top, prep players in the whole country.

Meanwhile, his alma mater, Oak Hill Academy, went into the finals with an incredible winning streak of 42 straight games. They participated in the Les Schwab Invitational, and Anthony won tournament MVP honors. This was only the beginning of the high school's postseason success. They went on to win two more major tournaments including the Nike Academy National Invitational. Up next was the highly anticipated game against St. Vincent-St. Mary High School in Akron, Ohio. In that hyped up game, he was matched up with fellow high school star and good friend LeBron James. While LeBron scored 36 points, Anthony piled up 34 points and 11 rebounds on his way to leading his team to the victory. Oak Hill ended the season ranked third in the country at 32–1. Anthony was on fire, but could he keep the flames burning at Syracuse?

Chapter 3: College Years at Syracuse

Anthony continued carving out his basketball legacy as a freshman at Syracuse University. Back then, there were no pundits or fans who believed that a freshman could make any meaningful moves that could significantly transform the unranked Syracuse team. After all, you do not see many rookie players who can instantly turn a mediocre team into championship contenders. However, Melo was not just some player. He was a scoring prodigy and one of the top prep prospects in the whole nation. Moreover, he had an excellent supporting cast composed of future NBA players Hakim Warrick, a power forward with explosive hops, and Kueth Duany, who was the Orangemen's leader.

Syracuse opened the season against Memphis in New York's Madison Square Garden, a neutral territory, but they lost 70-63. The freshman Anthony, however, was superb, playing all 40 minutes while scoring 27 points and grabbing 11 rebounds. Impressive for his first collegiate game. The AP game report called Anthony a "one-man show" and prophetically noted that he appeared at home under the bright lights of Madison Square Garden.

What was not prophesied was the success of the Orangemen after the opening-day setback. Syracuse accomplished 11 straight wins, including victories over Georgia Tech, Seton Hall, Boston College, and Missouri. Anthony scored at least 20 points in all but two of the 11 matches. By the end of the winning streak, the Orangemen were ranked 25th in the AP poll. Not only had Anthony transformed the team overnight, but he also changed the minds of skeptics who doubted what he could do.

Anthony was identified as a threat. Pick a spot on the court, and he could land a shot from there. After almost 30 years on the job, even Coach Boeheim admitted that he was often astounded by Anthony's skills. Even so, that did not mean that Anthony's single year at Syracuse was flawless. In mid-January, in the game against Pittsburgh and the third Big East game of the season, the Panthers' veterans exposed the rookie, Anthony, to experience that he had not experienced before on the court. They managed to restrict the forward to just 14 points and a season-low three rebounds, easily beating the Orangemen 73-60. Jaron Brown, in particular, defended Anthony relentlessly and prevented him from playing the scoring game to which fans had become accustomed. This was a big deal for Brown. He trash-talked, bragging, "We're a physical team, and he wore down quicker than I thought he would."

Anthony used those words as motivation and encouragement to grind harder. In the rematch two weeks later, Anthony again scored 14 points, but this time, he had a game-high of 13 rebounds. The Syracuse Orangemen snatched the win from the second-ranked Panthers, 67-65. Other close calls included an 82-80 win over No. 10 Notre Dame, where Anthony scored ten on a 14-2 run, eliminating a 12-point deficit and tying the game at 69-69 with 6.5 minutes left. Two games later, his three-point play gave Syracuse another marginal, yet significant victory in a 76-75 win at Michigan State, which was one of the only five home losses for the Spartans that year.

Syracuse had never won a men's basketball national championship when Anthony came on the scene, and few expected that to change anytime soon. His first and only year at Syracuse between 2002 and 2003 was groundbreaking. Anthony normed 22.2 points and ten rebounds as a rookie. He virtually led the Syracuse Orangemen in every category whether it was scoring, rebounding, minutes played, or free throws. With him leading the way, Syracuse was a third seed entering March Madness.

This made a big difference against Oklahoma in the Elite Eight. Anthony began setting new records, like his 33-point explosion in Syracuse's Final Four win over Player of the Year T.J. Ford and the Texas Longhorns. His explosion was a record for most points scored by a rookie in the NCAA tournament. For the national title, Syracuse faced the University of Kansas, another perennial NCAA powerhouse team. In that game, Anthony had 20 points and ten rebounds. The Orangemen ended up winning the game and title while Anthony was the best player in March Madness. Another of Anthony's accomplishments in college included being named AP Second-Team All-American. Anthony's showing on the court secured his name for NCAA Freshman of the Year, All-Big East First Team, and the Big East Conference Freshman of the Year.

Although NBA scouts flocked to see him play, Anthony managed to stay focused on his game, shining like an experienced star. Hence, the man-among-boys cliché did not describe Anthony's college days. Anthony was still a developing work in progress, growing into the frame that would one day make him a low-post nightmare for less vertically-blessed NBA forwards. Compared to other recent freshmen stars at the time, Anthony's size and athleticism were not as impressive as his unearthly basketball penetration. Contrary to the criticism he would later receive in the NBA, commentators glorified Anthony's unselfishness and praised his unique sense for the game. His willingness to trust teammates with the ball at times when he was taking the heat was evident every night in the scores.

Back then, Syracuse had four players averaging in double figures. Division I may have seen its share of great freshmen athletes, but Anthony was a fantastic rookie leader who had closed the gap by elevating his team with his vigor and all-around proficiency. Anthony's leadership among his teammates during the NCAA title game resulted in an 81-78 victory over Kansas. Teammates like guard Gerry McNamara felt that Anthony played well with the team and was impressed with the fact that such a great scorer could play alongside other guys in a supportive fashion. Assistant coach Troy Weaver, who recruited Anthony, thought that he brought a calming demeanor to the team, noting, "When the best player is relaxed, not tense and not pressured, it relaxes everybody else."

Besides getting him recognized in all the news sources, Anthony's performance in the Final Four did something else. It ensured a top selection in the 2003 NBA Draft. The initial plan, according to Anthony, was for a two to three-season run at Syracuse. However, having accomplished and exceeded all of his goals, he decided to suspend his college career and declared himself eligible for the 2003 NBA Draft. Coach Boeheim supported his decision. Melo told Boeheim that he wanted to win a title with Syracuse in his college stint. However, he did so in just his freshman season, and there was nothing left for him to do but to go to the NBA.

Though he only completed one season, Anthony had broken new ground by taking the Syracuse route, and younger players were taking note. Other top high school prospects were intrigued by Anthony's dominance. They began to reconsider the value of a brief layover on a college court. NBA officials also took notice as Anthony's one-year college stop served to shape future eligibility requirements.

Chapter 4: Carmelo's NBA Career

Getting Drafted: The Infamous 2003 Draft Class

Carmelo Anthony enjoyed a single incredible college season. He led the Syracuse Orangemen in scoring and rebounding and was a virtual 20-10 guy in scoring and rebounding. The Orangemen went from being an unheralded team to one of the contenders for the NCAA title. With Carmelo, Syracuse enjoyed a good run in the NCAA tournament to become the national champions. It was all thanks to Melo, and the lanky forward was one of the best up-and-coming youngsters in the world.

As unbelievable as his college career was, and as good of an NBA prospect that he was, Anthony was not the top prospect in the 2003 Draft. Most of the attention went to the bullish 18-year-old kid from Ohio named LeBron James. LeBron, even as a high schooler, was gaining unprecedented national attention and was the most anticipated rookie of the 2003 Draft. He was the consensus top overall pick. That left Anthony as probably the second best pick in the draft. There were even questions about whether he was the second best player in the draft class that year.

The 2003 Draft class also had the likes of college veteran shooting guard Dwyane Wade out of Marquette, long and lanky versatile big man Chris Bosh, and 7-foot Serbian center Darko Miličić. There were even capable guys like Kirk Hinrich and Chris Kaman among others waiting to line up for their names to get called early in the first round. The 2003 NBA Draft was shaping up to be one of the best and most extensive classes in NBA history. Had Melo joined the draft a year later, or even the season earlier, he would have undoubtedly been the consensus top pick.

Nevertheless, Carmelo Anthony was a sure top-five pick in the draft and was at least a lottery pick. Melo had an unparalleled scoring ability for a college kid. He came into the draft as a near 6'8" small forward with a skinny frame. Despite being thin, Anthony seemed stronger than he looked, as he could bully his way to the basket from time to time. On top of that, his 41-inch vertical was also something to look forward to in a league that was continuing to get more athletic.

What was surprising about Carmelo Anthony was that, for a small forward, he had great handles. He could handle the ball with grace and lose opposing defenses with crossover moves and with one quick dribble going to the right. This was probably because of his initial training as a point guard when he was very young.

Another aspect of his game that he probably got from his point guard days was his shooting. Melo's shooting form always looked fluid and graceful. He could hit that jump shot from anywhere on the perimeter, and it remained one of his best weapons off the dribble during his college days. While many small forwards camped out on the three-point line or tried to bully their way to the basket, Melo had the ball in his hands and could dribble drive or pull up from anywhere on the perimeter. His 7-foot wingspan also contributes to his ability to shoot over opposing defenses.

Carmelo Anthony was also deceptively athletic. He could not jump out of the gym as high as fellow draft prospect LeBron James. He also did not run as fast as guards did. However, Melo used whatever athletic ability he had to the best he can. He has always had a swift first step that he often uses to get to the basket. When going up for a layup attempt, Anthony goes up powerfully and explosively, though he has never been a very big forward. His offensive game is just naturally fluid and graceful.

It is as if Melo was born with a natural feel for the game of basketball, unseen by even some of the veteran NBA players. Carmelo Anthony was arguably the most offensively gifted player in the 2003 NBA Draft. Nobody came close to his ability to score a basket. Not even the prodigy LeBron James, at that point in their respective careers, could contend with Melo as far as putting the ball in the basket was concerned. Carmelo Anthony was buckets reincarnated.[iii]

Other than his offense, his rebounding was also a good part of his game. Melo was a virtual double-double guy in college because of his ability to rebound. As previously stated, he was never the most athletic guy, nor the biggest person on the court. But he knew how to use his athletic gifts, and he knew how to use whatever size was given to him to rebound the ball very well. Despite his lanky frame, he was strong enough to bully his way for good positioning. He just had a nose for the ball.[iv]

Melo was an excellent prospect coming out of Syracuse. But there were aspects of his game that prevented him from being the best of the class. First off, Carmelo Anthony has never been a very impactful defensive player, even to this day. As good as he is on offense, he is just as bad on the other end of the court. It seems as if he puts all of his energy and basketball emphasis on the offensive side of the game and fails to put effort on defense.

It is not as if he lacks the tools to be an excellent defensive player; Melo is faster than most forwards are and has long arms. His athletic gifts would allow him to stay on the ball with his defensive assignments, and his wingspan could make him excellent in contesting shots or even blocking attempts at the basket. Anthony has all the tools to be good at the defensive end of the court, he probably just does not want to be.[v]

One other thing that has always been a knock on Carmelo's game was that he is so offensively gifted. When players become so good on offense and when they get into a good scoring zone, they sometimes forget that they have four other teammates on the floor. Melo is one of those players. Whenever he gets into the zone offensively, he begins to lose sight of his other teammates and freezes them out of the game. Being a confident scorer is usually a good trait to have, but being too cocky may get your team into trouble. Anthony can get so overconfident at times that he feels any shot he takes will go in when, in fact, they might be very dangerous shots. Hence, his shot selection has always needed to improve.

For a player that always had the ball in his hands to become active, Carmelo Anthony was never the best at making plays for his teammates. Whenever Melo decided to go to the basket, his mindset was always to score the ball despite the defense adjusting to him. He never seemed like the type of player that had the innate knack for finding open teammates. For a guy that attracted a lot of defensive attention, Carmelo Anthony should have developed the skills of making plays for other players. However, it seemed like that part of his game was still left to be honed.

Lastly, the most prominent thing lacking in Carmelo's offensive game is his decision-making whenever he would make plays for others. That was an aspect that made LeBron a better prospect than Melo. James already had that innate ability to make sound decisions in playmaking on top of his natural passing skills. While Anthony showed stretches where he could make good passes, his decision-making was never top notch. He sometimes attempts difficult passes that result in turnovers. There have also been instances when Melo cannot decide on moving the ball if he feels like he could not make passes. Those situations often led to broken offensive stretches.

While Carmelo Anthony was never a great all-around player, and while his defensive effort was sorely lacking early into his basketball career, there was no doubt in anyone's mind how gifted a scorer he was. Scoring is the name of the game, and there was nobody in the 2003 Draft class who did it better than Melo. Decision-making and defensive effort can be instilled during an NBA career. But the natural ability and instinct to score is often inborn and might not be as easy to teach as defense.

Based on scoring ability alone, Carmelo Anthony was undoubtedly one of the top picks of the draft, and anyone who passes on him might be crazy. LeBron James had all the athleticism in the world to dominate the league with his physical gifts alone, but he was often heralded for his all-around game rather than his scoring skills. Even Dwyane Wade, a scoring prodigy at Marquette, did not have the offensive versatility that Carmelo Anthony had. There was indeed no doubt that Anthony's ability to score the basket was at the top of the draft class and could even be among the best in the NBA.

Anthony officially became an NBA player on draft night of 2003 when he was selected third overall by the Denver Nuggets. Before this, the Denver Nuggets had trudged through a string of bad luck. They went into the draft tied for last, and ironically, the bad luck continued when they missed the pick for the top spot, or so it seemed.

The first pick in the draft went to the Cleveland Cavaliers, who picked hometown kid LeBron James, to nobody's surprise. The second went to the Detroit Pistons, who selected the big man

Darko Miličić. Many were surprised by that pick, but the Pistons knew what they were doing despite Darko not being able to develop into a superb NBA player. Detroit already had a small forward named Tayshaun Prince, whom they were grooming for a possible championship run with the team. Meanwhile, Darko seemed like a prospect that would develop into a hybrid player in the NBA. He never did.

Seeing as how the best prospect was already chosen and how the Pistons had passed on Carmelo Anthony, the Nuggets were elated to see arguably the second best player of the class still available for drafting aside from all the other good prospects in the draft. Also, even if the Pistons took Melo, the market would prove profitable, regardless of all the other talent in that pool. The Nuggets were still able to get an up-and-coming superstar. Incredible as it may seem, that single draft pick changed the historical culture of losing in Denver. The incredible talent of Anthony will be a topic of debate for years to come. The facts, however, speak for themselves. One point is that the Nuggets picked Anthony, who was prophesied to become an icon even before he bounced a ball on an NBA court, and this changed everything for the Denver Nuggets.

Rookie Season

Melo was joining a Denver Nuggets team coached by Jeff Bzdelik, who was later replaced by the legendary George Karl. Though the team had been struggling before his arrival, Carmelo Anthony was intent on being the catalyst for changing the culture of the Nuggets. Denver had a few veterans on the team in the likes of Andre Miller, Marcus Camby, and Earl Boykins. The Nuggets had a few capable players who could make plays for others and defend at a high level, but they lacked scoring. That was what Melo could provide to any team.

For Carmelo's NBA debut, the Nuggets faced the San Antonio Spurs in their first game of the season on October 29, 2003, and started the season with a win, upsetting the defending NBA champions 80-72. The rookie forward scored only 12 points in that game on a weak 4 out of 15 clip from the floor. Nevertheless, he had seven rebounds in that win against the defensive-minded Spurs. The lights came back on, and the magic returned to Denver. They had a new attitude, inspired by the hope that Anthony brought to the franchise.

Melo's breakout game as a rookie NBA player was against the Sacramento Kings, another playoff team, in his third game. He had 23 points, six rebounds, and five assists in that blowout win for the Nuggets on November 1. From then on, it was evident that Carmelo Anthony's star was beginning to rise despite scoring only 2 points in his next game.

Out of nowhere, the Nuggets began digging themselves out of the pathetic losing run that had plagued them for years. The Nuggets had been the butt of many NBA jokes for years, but now they were starting to appear on national television again. They gained buzz as a dangerous team, and the transformation was beginning. In only his sixth NBA game, Anthony scored 30 points. With that, he became the youngest NBA player next to Kobe Bryant to score 30 or more points.

A week after scoring 30 points, Carmelo Anthony would add another highlight to his already bright rookie resume. He would grab 14 big rebounds along with his 17 points and seven assists in a win over the Orlando Magic. Melo was showing that he was not only a scoring machine, but a reliable player on the rebounding end as well. He would have five double-doubles on scoring and rebounding in just his first 20 games.

On December 26, Carmelo Anthony would eclipse his 30-point performance by putting up 37 points in a narrow win against the Houston Rockets. He made five three-pointers in that game and was displaying his full arsenal on the offensive end. He then became the third-youngest player to score 1,000 points in his career. Carmelo did that against the Memphis Grizzlies during February of 2004. That was only one week after he scored a new career-high of 39 in a win against the Portland Trailblazers. He would score 30 or more points two more times in February. Carmelo Anthony was also one of the privileged rookies to take part in the Rookie Challenge.

Late in March, Melo set a franchise record for most points scored by a rookie. He had 41 points against the Seattle SuperSonics. With those points, he was also the second youngest player to score 40 in a single game. After winning the Rookie of the Month Award for the Western Conference in April, Anthony completed a sweep of all the Western Conference Rookie of the Month Awards. It was only the fourth time that such a feat was achieved.

In a stellar rookie season, Carmelo Anthony started in all 82 regular-season games and averaged 21.0 points, 6.1 rebounds, 2.8 assists, and 1.2 steals. Anthony was the highest scoring rookie that season. He lifted the Nuggets to a 43–39 overall record and into a first-round playoff position against the Minnesota Timberwolves. The Nuggets had a massive lift after hiring Karl as the head coach. They went on to win 32 of their next 40 games once George Karl took the reins.

Anthony finished second to LeBron James of the Cleveland Cavaliers in voting for the 2003-2004 NBA Rookie of the Year Award. Many felt that he was robbed, seeing that the Nuggets secured a spot in the playoffs and the Cavaliers did not. Melo had better scoring numbers than LeBron, but the latter won the award due to his all-around ability, which was something that Melo needed to work on. The fact that LeBron James also gained most of the national media's attention even hurt Melo's bid for the award.

Carmelo Anthony and the Denver Nuggets went on to face the Timberwolves in the first round. The Wolves were the top-seeded team in the Western Conference and were led by the MVP Kevin Garnett. Melo had to pull out all the stops to compete well with the better team.

Game 1 started, and Carmelo Anthony was off to his first-ever playoff series in only his rookie season. It seemed to be a similar scenario to that of his lone season in Syracuse. The Orangemen were not NCAA favorites before Melo's arrival, but Anthony was able to lead them to the national title. In Denver's case, they suffered years of obscurity before drafting Melo. But when the lanky small forward joined the team, the culture suddenly changed, and it seemed like they were on their way to a winning tradition.

Unfortunately, his first playoff game did not go well. The Nuggets lost to the Wolves despite Carmelo Anthony posting good numbers for a rookie. He had 19 points and six rebounds for the losing team. After losing Game 1 by 14 points, the Nuggets lost Game 2 by 15 before moving back to Denver for Game 3. The third game of the series was a lot different from the first two games. Carmelo Anthony had a double-double performance with 24 points and ten rebounds, and the Nuggets led the game from start to finish as they blew the Wolves out with a 21-point win.

However, that was the best that the Denver Nuggets performed in the playoffs. They put up a good fight in Game 4 after playing toe-to-toe with the Wolves from the opening tip. Unfortunately, their lack of experience got the best of them as they failed to perform and defend down the stretch to lose it by merely 2 points. Back in Minnesota, the Wolves closed out the series, 102 to 91. In Denver's case, it was a valiant effort in their return to the playoffs, but they were just a tad too inexperienced. Even their best player, who only had 2 points on 1 out of 16 shooting, was still also lacking in the experience department.

Carmelo Anthony had one of the best rookie seasons anyone could expect from a first-year player. He was the first rookie player to lead a playoff team in scoring since David Robinson of the Spurs more than a decade earlier. It was also a baptism of fire for the young Melo, as he was able to get to the playoffs to face the best team in the West. Though his rookie season was cut short by the first-round exit, Melo was just thankful for the playoff experience that not a lot of rookies get. Anthony then played for the U.S. basketball team at the 2004 Summer Olympics. However, he did not have a solid game and spent much of the time on the bench, with the US settling for the Bronze Medal that year.

Second Season

Coming into their second season with Carmelo Anthony in the lineup, the Denver Nuggets did not change a lot about their core roster. The only significant addition to the lineup was a former All-Star power forward Kenyon Martin, who was traded from the New Jersey Nets in exchange for three draft picks. They also drafted Jarrett Jack, who was immediately traded to the Portland Trail Blazers for Lithuanian rookie shooter Linas Kleiza. Though there were no significant roster changes, the more important things were that George Karl was in for a full season and that Melo was a year better and wiser.

Carmelo Anthony immediately made an impact in his second year by continuing his torrid scoring pace. He became the third-youngest player in league history to reach 2,000 career points during a game against Miami early in December 2004. Only two players in league history had scored 2,000 career points at younger ages. The first one was Kobe Bryant back in his teenage years, and the second one was LeBron James, who had accomplished the feat a few games earlier than Melo. James achieved it in 92 games whereas Anthony got to 2,000 points in his 97th career game. Though Melo is the third youngest in that feat, he was the second-fastest to reach that milestone since Kobe needed to play 162 games to get to 2,000 points.vi

With Carmelo leading the Nuggets once again in scoring in only his second season in the league, he was selected to participate in the Rookie Challenge as a member of the sophomore team together with the likes of LeBron James, Dwyane Wade, and Chris Bosh. Though that squad was full of talent, Anthony was the brightest star that night as he led the team with 31 big points in a 27-point blowout victory over the rookies. He shot 13 of 18 from the field and was the Most Valuable Player of that exhibition game.

Carmelo Anthony ended the regular season by averaging 20.8 points, 5.7 rebounds, and 2.6 assists per game. His numbers were a little bit lower than his rookie numbers, but he did play almost two minutes less and shot about 5% better than he had the previous season. He also scored at least 10 points in all of his 75 games except for seven of them. More importantly, the Denver Nuggets improved their regular season win-loss record to 49-33—a 6-game improvement from Melo's rookie season. His team also promoted a seed higher and went into the playoffs with the seventh seed.

Unfortunately, the Nuggets faced one of the best teams in the league—the San Antonio Spurs. Led by two-time league MVP and defensive stalwart Tim Duncan, the Spurs were a ferocious defensive team that could shut down almost any high-scoring athlete in the game. With Melo as the team's lone bright spot on the offensive end, the Nuggets needed its other players to step up and take a lot of scoring load off their star forward.

Andre Miller did just that in Game 1. With the Spurs' defense focusing on the second-year player, Miller took the scoring reins to lead a fourth-quarter rally against the mighty Spurs. They played their brand of tough defense in the final canto of the game by limiting the Spurs to only 12 points. Miller scored a game-high 31 points. The Nuggets were elated to have stolen home-court advantage away from the Spurs. Unfortunately, that was their best output that year. The Spurs shut down every Nuggets player in Game 2, including Melo. The highest-scoring Denver player was role player DerMarr Johnson with 12 points.

Meanwhile, Tim Duncan scored 24 points to lead a balanced offense on the way to a 104-76 victory over San Antonio.

Game 3 was no different even though the Nuggets were on their home floor. Though it was a tighter game than Game 2, the Spurs were still able to hold on to the match, as Manu Ginobili scored 32 points off the bench. Meanwhile, Melo had one of his better playoff games that season with 19 points. In Game 4, Denver fought the Spurs tooth and nail as they entered the fourth quarter with a 7-point lead. However, the San Antonio squad battled back to tie the game and send it to overtime. As the Nuggets were a very inexperienced team, they could muster up only eight overtime points to the 19 of the Spurs. In the end, they fell a game short of elimination. The Nuggets did not seem desperate in extending their postseason appearance, as the Spurs won every quarter in Game 5 except the second to win the series in five games. Carmelo Anthony scored 25 in that match, but it was in a losing effort.

With his second season in the NBA all but over, Carmelo Anthony seemed like the lone bright spot on the offensive end for the Denver Nuggets. They had good defenders and rebounders like Marcus Camby and Kenyon Martin. Their playmakers were not bad, either. Andre Miller and Earl Boykins were capable point guards in their rights, but the only consistent scorer was Melo. He apparently needed a lot of help. But if the Nuggets were not willing to give him the help he needed, Carmelo Anthony would just have to score a lot more points.

Rising Star Scorer

The Denver Nuggets kept their core players intact. Andre Miller was still running the point while the front line was manned by shot-blocking expert Marcus Camby and athletic power forward Kenyon Martin. Most important of all, Carmelo Anthony was always their best player and scorer. Unfortunately, management did not do enough to get help for their rising forward. Melo did not get the scoring help he needed, so he decided to make himself a better scorer instead.

Anthony started the season at a terrific scoring pace. He would not relent at putting points up on the board. The rising third-year player out of Syracuse scored in double digits in all but one of his first 20 games for the 2005-06 season. Carmelo Anthony even had a 40-point output in that span of games in a win against the Miami Heat and draft-mate Dwyane Wade. Two games later, he would score 42 in a win over Charlotte.

Carmelo Anthony was scoring at a higher pace than he ever had in his three-year career. He had many games where he scored more than 30 points. Melo also had four 40-point outputs that season, including a then career-high of 45 points against the Philadelphia 76ers in a loss late in December 2005. He then reached the 5,000-point barrier when he scored 33 points in a loss to the Memphis Grizzlies. Anthony became the second youngest player in NBA history to reach 5,000 career points. The youngest was, once again, LeBron James.

Melo's torrid scoring rate did not stop there. He would have 43 points and 11 rebounds in 51 minutes in an overtime win over the Phoenix Suns on January 10, 2006. That was arguably his best performance in his young NBA career at that point. Anthony was also one of the best clutch performers of the 2005-06 NBA season. He was able to hit five shots to win games on different occasions. What was even more amazing is that those game-winners were all perimeter shots, which were testaments to how much Carmelo Anthony had refined his jump-shooting touch on the perimeter. Though Anthony was a much-improved scorer and even better primetime performer, he was not chosen as an All-Star for the Western Conference that year. The West was loaded with talented wings at that time with the likes of Kobe Bryant, Tracy McGrady, Ray Allen, and Shawn Marion. Even though he was not an All-Star, it seemed a travesty that a player of Melo's talents was not included.

In his third season in the NBA, Carmelo Anthony had nearly perfect attendance during 2005-2006, playing in all but two games in the 82-game schedule. He averaged 26.5 points, 2.7 assists, and 4.9 rebounds per game. He was in the top 10 in scoring in the league and was one of the most improved scorers, raising his scoring average by almost 6 points per game. Most importantly, he was more efficient in scoring, though he was shooting the ball at a higher rate. His field goal percentage was at a then career-high of 48%, which was a 5% increase from his second year.

In a time when some of the best scorers the league has ever seen (Kobe Bryant, Allen Iverson, LeBron James, Paul Pierce, Dwyane Wade, and Dirk Nowitzki) were at the prime years of their scoring prowess, Carmelo Anthony's ability to put up points in a hurry was not far behind. At the end of the regular season, he was eighth overall in points per game in what turned out to be a high-scoring NBA season.

Aside from scoring at least 30 points in 28 of 80 games he played, Melo also became only the second Nugget to rank among the top 10 scorers since Michael Adams did it in 1991. He was also selected as a member of the All-NBA Third Team. That was his first All-NBA selection. Go back two months from that point in time, and voters would have probably questioned themselves for not putting Carmelo Anthony in the All-Star game.

At the conclusion of the season, the Denver Nuggets shined just a little brighter by finishing in third place. Though they had a mediocre win-loss record of 44-38, they were the third seed in the West by their top finish in their division. They were headed to face the Los Angeles Clippers in the first round. But since the Clippers had a better regular season record, they were given the home-court advantage to the dismay of the Nuggets. The Clips were skilled enough to win a close Game 1 on their home floor even after a big fourth-quarter rally by the Nuggets. Melo finished that losing effort with 25 points.

In Game 2, Melo was limited to just 16 points by the Clipper defense, and the LA-based squad went on to a 2-0 advantage over their foes. The Nuggets were not so lucky at home. They won Game 3 and lost Game 4. Anthony was their lone bright spot on offense once again as he scored 24 in their winning effort, but only 17 when they lost in Game 4. The losing streak continued back in Los Angeles when Denver lost Game 5, thus eliminating the Nuggets from the playoffs. Melo only scored 17 and 23 in those games as the Clipper defense converged on the only good scorer that the Nuggets had. By the conclusion of the Nuggets' third straight first-round exit, Anthony averaged 21 points on a dismal 33% from the floor. It was clear that he needed help to win more playoff games. However, not all was lost in Anthony's world. Recognizing the benefit of Anthony to the Denver Nuggets franchise, he was offered a 5-year, $80 million extension.

All-Star Status, Partnership with Allen Iverson

With Denver not getting anywhere with their lineup, the Nuggets management did not renew Kiki Vandeweghe's contract as the team's general manager, probably for failing to form a stable cast around Anthony. He was replaced by Mark Warkentien. Once again, the Nuggets kept their core lineup intact at the start of the season. The only difference was the addition of mercurial scoring wingman JR Smith, who was acquired in an offseason trade.

With no apparent significant changes in their lineup at the start of the season, it was becoming more evident that the rising forward from Syracuse would shoulder the majority of the scoring load for the Denver Nuggets once more. Though the coaching and Carmelo Anthony's scoring prowess were enough to take them into the playoffs, it was clear that the Denver Nuggets needed more than their superstar could offer.

Nevertheless, early in the 2006–2007 season, Carmelo Anthony recorded six straight games of scoring more than 30 points. He was able to tie a Denver record by doing so. Unfortunately, the streak was broken soon after when he scored only 29 in the next game versus the Chicago Bulls. With his skill for making shots, Anthony started his streak again and went on to score 30 or more points in six straight outings. Unfortunately, he once again failed in the task of breaking that franchise record.

Ten days later, he was involved in a brawl during a game against the New York Knicks. The incident occurred in the last seconds of the Knicks' home game in the middle of December, when the Nuggets led 119–100. The initial altercation was just a routine hard foul between Mardy Collins and JR Smith, but it quickly escalated into a full-blown melee. News sources flooded the media with clips of Anthony serving New York's Mardy Collins with a sucker punch to the face. Many compared this fight to the Pacers-Pistons brawl two years earlier, noting the only difference was that during the former, players went into the stands and fought with fans.

NBA commissioner David Stern suspended seven players without pay for 47 games, and Anthony was among them. For his actions, he received a 15-game suspension. David Stern and the NBA were highly criticized for being excessive because this altercation was one of the most penalized on-court fights in the league. Commentators claimed the league used the players to set an example to clean up its image from the Pacers-Pistons fight. They wanted to send the message that these streetball antics would not be tolerated. Anthony was criticized for tarnishing his image as a rising star. The day after, Anthony issued an apology to his family, fans, the league, and specifically Collins.

In the midst of the brawl and suspensions drama, the Nuggets made a trade that changed their fortunes from then on. Even though Anthony, who was serving his suspension at that time, could play all 82 games during the regular season and owned the majority of the team's offensive burden, but there was only so much weight that his young and inexperienced shoulders could carry despite his undeniable talent in scoring the basketball. He needed help fast before his patience would run out.

By acquiring Philadelphia's bad boy Allen Iverson in exchange for Nuggets point guard Andre Miller and several first-round picks, Carmelo Anthony finally had a partner that loved putting up points just as much as he did. For his part, Iverson was unhappy in Philadelphia for their failure to deliver a reliable supporting cast. He was winning scoring titles along with an MVP in Philly. However, his one-man show in that part of the country never translated into anything more than a lone Finals appearance in 2001.

The trade was supposed to be good for both teams, as the 76ers were able to get rid of Iverson, who was a distraction for the team, while the Nuggets were able to get another scoring option besides Anthony. With Allen Iverson in the fold, the Denver Nuggets no longer needed to rely on Melo's solo act. They had a solid one-two punch on the scoring end, enough to strike fear in the hearts of all of their opponents.

However, due to the suspensions, the pair did not get to coordinate their skills on the court until the game against the Memphis Grizzlies in January 2007. On that day, Anthony made his return from the suspension. Never in Anthony's three-plus seasons in Denver had the Nuggets been better equipped to become one of the NBA's best teams.

When Iverson was traded, Anthony was leading the NBA in scoring at 31.6 points a game. Iverson was number 2 at 31.2. Still, many questions preceded the matchup. Could Iverson and Anthony co-exist? Could either of them play a more team-oriented offense? Would the two dominant scorers be able to share possessions well enough to give the Nuggets a fluid offense? Could any of the Nuggets play the championship-caliber defense needed to be a successful franchise and a formidable opponent?

Such questions were all legitimate queries. Allen Iverson was never known to be a team player back in his days with the Philadelphia 76ers. He was an MVP that never saw a shot he did not like. However, he was the type of player that always needed the ball in his hands to become active whether when he was calling his shots or passing off to teammates.

Despite being nearly nine inches taller and about 70 pounds heavier playing the forward position, Carmelo Anthony was not an entirely different player from Iverson. Anthony could put the ball through the hoop from no matter the distance, angle, or situation. His ability to score the basket was as complete as it could get. But, like AI, he always needed possession of the ball to become active. Everything on offense revolved around him. It was the same situation with Iverson back when he was in Philly. Thus, it was easy to question how such a partnership could prosper because there was only one ball to move around for two scoring superstars.

The Anthony-Iverson combo would nevertheless succeed in their first game as a duo. In that game against the Memphis Grizzlies, whom the Nuggets beat by 17 points, Carmelo

Anthony delivered 28 points, five rebounds, and six assists. Iverson was not too shabby himself, scoring 23 points while attempting only 16 shots to get his new partner back into game shape.

Even with the presence of a multiple-time scoring champion in the form of Iverson in Denver, Carmelo Anthony was still the Nuggets' leading man as the season went on. After that 28-point output versus Memphis, Melo sizzled for a combined 71 points in the next two games while he and AI were just starting to scratch the surface of their partnership.

The scoring barrage for Carmelo Anthony would not stop. Not only was he norming about 30 points with Iverson attracting defenses, but he was also looking like Magic Johnson out there because of the well-roundedness of his game. He would have his first triple-double on February 5 against the Phoenix Suns. Melo had 31 points, ten rebounds, and ten assists in that match. Nevertheless, the deadly scoring duo was not yet coordinated. They were losing more than they were winning.

Anthony had accomplished a great deal in only a short time and had his eyes set on a spot on the All-Star team. However, Carmelo was overlooked by the All-Star voters yet again. It was another travesty. Anthony was playing even better than the previous season. With the points he was putting up on the board and how he was leading the Denver Nuggets through a tough Western Conference, how could he not be an All-Star starter?

However, as fate would have it, two spots opened up due to injuries to two All-Stars. Then-NBA commissioner David Stern did not make a mistake in naming Carmelo Anthony as one of the replacements for the injured players. The 22-year-old superstar forward was finally an All-Star after three seasons of being snubbed. Anthony did not disappoint in his first appearance, recording 20 points and nine rebounds in his All-Star debut. It was also the first time in a very long time that the Denver Nuggets had two All-Stars. Iverson was also selected to that event for the eighth overall time.

Anthony excelled in his game and continued carving out his legacy in the NBA. Despite a rocky start to their partnership of wearing powder blue uniforms, Melo and AI would look better as a duo by March of that season after adjusting well to each other's games and tendencies. While Anthony was still the Nuggets' leading man, Iverson did not disappoint in giving Denver a reliable second scoring option. The two superstars would finally fulfill their potential as possibly the best scoring tandem in the NBA.

Denver only lost one out of 11 games in April thanks to Melo's leadership. After all was said and done in the regular season, Carmelo Anthony averaged 28.9 points, which were merely second overall to Kobe Bryant that year. After barely cracking the top 10 in scoring the previous season, Carmelo Anthony was the NBA's second best that year. He could have even been the best if he did not need to share the ball with Iverson so much. However, it was best for the Nuggets to have another scorer in the form of Allen Iverson.

Carmelo Anthony also averaged 6.0 rebounds and 3.8 assists. He was also named to the All-NBA Third Team. For a second time in his career, Melo was included among the fifteen best players in the NBA. Carmelo Anthony was quickly becoming one of the league's best young players and was increasing his scoring averages while helping his team win games. With the addition of Allen Iverson to the lineup, the Denver Nuggets won 45 games in the regular season.

Back on the court, it was déjà vu when Anthony and the Nuggets faced the San Antonio Spurs, who would become the eventual champions that year, in the first round of the playoffs. In what appeared to be a replica of their 2005 matchup, Denver won the first game in San Antonio, 95–89, only to drop the next four games. The Nuggets won Game 1 on the strength of

Iverson's 31 points. They lost the next four games even though Anthony scored well in all four of them. This was the fourth consecutive year the Nuggets were eliminated without making it through the first round. In the playoffs, Carmelo Anthony led the way for the Nuggets with 26.8 points and 8.6 boards.

Coming into the 2007-08 season, the Denver Nuggets were a hopeful squad with a complete roster as far as scoring the basketball was concerned. More importantly, Carmelo Anthony and Allen Iverson, who were Denver's best players, were going to be more fluid as a combo.

Showing that his explosive scoring year during the 2006-07 season was not a fluke, Carmelo Anthony opened the new season by scoring 32 and 33 in the Denver Nuggets' first two games, which were both wins. Then, he was the catalyst for the Nuggets when the team won six straight games early in the season to go up 8-3 in their first 11 outings. Five of those wins were blowouts. Anthony did not score less than 20 points during any game in that stretch.

Carmelo Anthony would then start an excellent four-game personal stretch in the middle of December 2007. He opened it up by recording 37 points and 16 rebounds in an overtime win over the Houston Rockets before finishing the next three games with consecutive point-rebound double-doubles. By scoring 29 points and securing ten rebounds in the fourth match, Melo barely missed four straight games of scoring at least 30 points and grabbing at least ten boards.

Scoring was the name of the game, and almost nobody in the league could do it better than Carmelo Anthony. His performance on February 8, 2008, was a testament to that fact. In that game against the Washington Wizards, it seemed like Melo could not miss no matter where he shot the ball from. He made 19 of his 25 field goal attempts and scored a career-best 49 points in only 39 minutes.

With his steady performance throughout the season, Anthony made his second consecutive appearance at an NBA All-Star Game. This time, he was not just a substitute. Not only did he make the team, but he was also a starter. He led in votes among Western Conference forwards, and less than 300,000 votes separated him from Kobe Bryant among all Western Conference players. He would score 18 points in his second All-Star game appearance and his first as a starter.

As an encore to his 49-point performance in February, Carmelo Anthony would outdo that output in April when the regular season was about to end. In 38 minutes of action against the

Sacramento Kings in a loss, Anthony scored 47 points and grabbed 11 rebounds. He made 19 of his 24 field goal attempts in that terrific performance. Melo would follow up that performance with 38 and 36 points in the next two games.

He finished the regular season having played in 77 games as the NBA's fourth-leading scorer with 25.7 points per game. He also had a then career-high in rebounding with 7.4 and shot his best percentage from the floor at 49.2%, thanks to his improved jump shot as well as the presence of scoring threats like Iverson and JR Smith. However, Carmelo Anthony did not lead the team in scoring for the first time in his five-year career. It was Iverson, who played more than 41 minutes a night, who led the Nuggets in scoring.

The Denver Nuggets would win their final game of the season against the Memphis Grizzlies. By winning that game, the Nuggets had officially won at least 50 games for the first time in the history of the franchise. At that moment, the 2007-08 Nuggets were the best incarnation of the franchise in history. Nevertheless, they would only make the playoffs as the eighth seed because the Western Conference was just getting more competitive.

At the start of the regular season, analysts were quick to suggest that the Denver Nuggets would make a quantum leap up the Western Conference standings, mainly because of the presence of two of the best scorers the league had ever seen in that era. However, they failed to reach expectations. Though the Nuggets were a dangerous bunch on offense, they desperately lacked in defense. Hence, they barely made the playoffs again.

Still, the 50-win season marked the highest win total for an eighth-seeded team in NBA history. This was a recipe for good basketball. In the first round, the Nuggets competed against the top-seeded Los Angeles Lakers. The fact that only seven games separated the top-seeded Lakers and the eighth-seeded Nuggets made it more exciting. Their margin of wins was the closest between a top seed and the eighth seed in NBA history. Because of that, it seemed like the Denver Nuggets had a fighting chance against the favorites in the West.

Anthony was obviously legitimate. He had proven himself many times over, but it was a different story for Marcus Camby and Kenyon Martin. The latter two Nuggets struggled throughout the season regarding health and effectiveness. In the playoffs, the Nuggets' performance was littered with flaws. There was no set offense. Effort from the defense was poor. Faltering from intimidation or lack of concentration, the players were off. They seemed to lack composure, rushed jump shots, over-dribbled, and stood cluelessly. Worst of all, they complained to the referees. Juxtaposed with the classy, serious, well-coached, and professional Lakers team, the Nuggets appeared to be out of their league.

But you could not blame the Nuggets for their lackluster effort in the playoffs. The Lakers were just too good a team that season, especially with Kobe Bryant winning the MVP award and new Laker Pau Gasol dominating his Nuggets matchup. Moreover, Lakers head coach Phil Jackson has had the number of Nuggets head coach George Karl ever since the glory days of the mid-90s. Apart from the Nuggets' confused performances, they were also unlucky to have met a Lakers team that they did not match up with well.

While it was easy to blame the other Nuggets for their lack of effort and the superiority of the Lakers as far as talent was concerned, one could also point out how Carmelo Anthony legitimately struggled in that series despite being one of the best scorers in the NBA during the regular season. Playing against his longtime idol Kobe Bryant for the first time in the postseason did not inspire him at all.

While Carmelo Anthony started Game 1 by scoring 30 points, it all went downhill from there. There was nothing he could do against the Laker defense, and he continued to struggle from the floor in the next three games, which were all definite losses. His worst performance was in Game 3 when he shot only 22.7% from the floor.

Because of that and in spite of the marginal success the Nuggets had been having in the regular season, the Lakers swept them in four games. These losses were historical because this was only the second time that the league had seen a 50-win team wiped out in a best-of-seven playoff series in the first round. Anthony only averaged 22.5 points per game and a then-career high of 9.5 rebounds per game in the playoffs.

But it seemed like Melo could not gel well with AI, who needed the ball just as much as he did. Despite leading Denver to the best season the franchise has ever seen, the duo of Carmelo Anthony and Allen Iverson was not enough to take them to higher planes. After that disappointing and embarrassing four-game loss to the Lakers, it seemed like it was all over for the short-lived high-scoring partnership of Anthony and Iverson.

End of the Anthony/Iverson Combo, Enter Anthony/Billups

Before the start of the 2008-09 season, the Nuggets decided to trade the 2007 Defensive Player of the Year, Marcus Camby, to the Clippers for a second-round draft pick. The deal seemed a little far-fetched and odd, especially considering that Camby was a player with defensive capabilities almost nobody else in the league could match. It was a clear sign that the Nuggets management wanted the team to go a different direction, especially since the trade freed a lot of salary cap space for future signings. The team was also poised to make another big deal because the Anthony/Iverson duo did not work as well as they had planned. It was clear that one of the two players had to go and Iverson, being the aging and declining star, was in the hot seat.

Thus, only a few games into the new season, Allen Iverson was immediately traded to the Detroit Pistons for All-Star point guard and NBA champion Chauncey Billups. Iverson merely played three games in the 2008-09 season, averaging just under 20 points per game. The decision was a shocker from Detroit's standpoint because Billups was so great of a point guard for the Pistons that he was arguably their best player since winning the championship back in 2004. For the Nuggets' part, they got rid of a player who was always a distraction for any team he had played for but was a once-in-a-lifetime offensive force in a little man's body. The trade made sense for Denver, as Billups was the playmaker and big shot maker that they needed to team up with Carmelo Anthony.

The trade signified the end of the short-lived partnership between Carmelo Anthony and Allen Iverson, who would go down in NBA history as two of the most celebrated scorers the league has ever seen. The trade allowed the Nuggets to start over with a new combo and to rebuild on what they had with Melo as the centerpiece of the offensive attack.

Despite the criticisms about how they played and how they did not have enough chemistry in their short stint together as teammates, Carmelo Anthony looked up to Allen Iverson and admired the way the little man played. Anthony grew up watching Iverson defy odds. He had always been a fan of the veteran scorer.

Fast-forward to several seasons later. Allen Iverson would be elected into the Naismith Basketball Hall of Fame. Of course, former teammate Carmelo Anthony was one of the few people to comment about AI. Anthony would say that he had always admired Iverson because of his toughness and perseverance. He stated that he and the best little man the league has ever seen share a common ground because of the way they both struggled from poverty to get to the point of success that they respectively achieved.[vii]

Carmelo Anthony was genuinely happy that his former teammate got the recognition he rightly deserved as a player. The toughness, perseverance, heart, and will to move forward were all traits that Iverson rubbed off on Anthony in a disappointingly short-lived partnership. Despite the short length of their stint as teammates, it was clear that Melo had learned all that he needed to from the multiple-time scoring champion and 11-time All-Star.

Going back to the 2008-09 season, Carmelo Anthony was ready to move forward from the Allen Iverson era in Denver. He was prepared to make the Nuggets his team again. Of course, he needed considerable help to do so, and Chauncey Billups was the right man for the job.

Unlike Iverson, Billups was a legitimate point guard that found pleasure in making plays for other teammates. He was also a champion. Though he did not take many shots, he only took those he believed he could hit. On top of that, most of those made shots were some of the biggest the NBA has ever seen, hence the nickname "Mr. Big Shot." Billups also added a lot of defensive versatility in the backcourt position. That was something that Iverson, despite his transcendent scoring prowess, did not have. The presence of Billups would only make things easier for a still-developing Carmelo Anthony.

Oddly, Carmelo Anthony did not start the season as the same scorer he was in the past two seasons. He was still the best player and scorer in Denver, but he was still adjusting to new teammates and defensive looks without Allen Iverson. Nevertheless, the Nuggets looked better than ever, and that was what mattered most. Guys like Billups, Nene, and Smith all had Melo's back during that struggle. But such a slump would not last long for a supreme scorer like Carmelo Anthony.

Early during December 2008 in a victory against the Minnesota Timberwolves, Melo made history by tying George Gervin's record for the most points in one quarter by scoring 33 points. It was a long-standing record and had been set more than three decades past already. Anthony's third-quarter explosion helped him get 45 points in that game. He also contributed with 11 rebounds that gave him a double-double that night. But in less than a month, Carmelo Anthony would be slowed down by a hand injury that he suffered against the Indiana Pacers.

The injury apparently bothered Carmelo Anthony more than he would admit. Though he was still scoring explosively from time-to-time, there were moments where he seemed like a fallen man because of the injury. He would struggle to put points up on the board while also finding it difficult to get himself into the scoring groove that had made him a famous athlete.

He had the hand splinted, opting to have his hand repaired using a less intrusive method with a quicker recovery time than surgery. A sore elbow had already sidelined him for three games in late December, and he was once again scheduled to miss several more games. Anthony's return came against the Charlotte Bobcats when he started and scored 19 points at the end of January 2009.

After returning from injury, Carmelo Anthony would quickly revert to the scoring form that had made him a deadly weapon from anywhere on the floor. He would score 35 points in his second game back while shooting 10 out of 17 in that win against the Spurs. After that, he looked like Steve Nash out there on the floor because of the 11 assists he dished out in a win against the OKC Thunder, even after scoring 32 points. What was even better than Melo's return to form was that the Denver Nuggets were rising faster than they ever had in franchise history. They were poised to break the 50-win mark they had set just a year back. That season, though, was not without controversy.

During a game against the Indiana Pacers, Anthony refused to leave the court after being told he was being benched. Some believe this incident was the first public sign of tension between himself and Coach Karl. His punishment was a one-game suspension. On top of that, Carmelo Anthony failed to get the recognition of the league because of the off-court and on-court struggles. Due to his injury and decreased overall play, Carmelo Anthony was not an All-Star that season.

The All-Star snub and the off-court issues did not seem to bother Melo, however, as the season progressed into the later months. Anthony was the catalyst in leading the Denver Nuggets to an eight-game winning streak from late March to early April. And in one of those wins, Carmelo Anthony scored 43 points and collected 11 rebounds versus the Dallas Mavericks. Just a day later, he put up 31 on the Warriors.

Despite Anthony's injuries and off-the-court issues with Karl, the Nuggets powered to a 54-28 win-loss record and the second seed in the ultra-competitive Western Conference. This was due to the leadership skills of Chauncey Billups as a veteran point guard with championship experience and to the improved play of players like Nene, JR Smith, and Chris "Birdman" Anderson, who became a crowd favorite in Denver. Just a season after recording a franchise-best in wins, the Nuggets outdid themselves by four wins in the 2008-09 season.

By the end of the 2008-09 season, Carmelo Anthony was still the team's leading scorer at 22.8 points per game. He shot lower percentages overall from the floor at about 44%, but his three-point shooting improved to 37%. Though Melo's scoring numbers were down from the previous seasons and were his lowest since his second year in the league, the Nuggets seemed to be a better team with Billups leading the way and with the role players stepping up big, primarily because the ball movement was better than ever.

The Denver Nuggets' first playoff opponents that year were the seventh-seeded New Orleans Hornets (now Pelicans). Just a season earlier, the Hornets had been in the same position as the Nuggets—the second best team in the West. The Hornets had Chris Paul, the best point guard in the NBA at that time, and it seemed like it would be a brutal first-round matchup. The Nuggets, however, had other plans in mind.

Carmelo Anthony's Nuggets opened the postseason strong by utterly obliterating the Hornets in Game 1. Melo was saddled with foul trouble early in the game and was limited to merely 13 points. However, their veteran playmaker exploded big. Chauncey Billups seemed as if he could not miss from beyond the arc when he converted a franchise playoff record of eight three-pointers on his way to 36 big points. It was a blowout victory, and the Nuggets won the game by 29 points. Game 2 was an encore for both the Nuggets and Billups. While Anthony had an efficient 22-point output on 10-of-20 shooting, Chauncey did a repeat of his Game 1 performance by converting four three-pointers to finish the game with 31 points as the Nuggets went on to a commanding 2-0 series lead with a 108-93 win.

While the Hornets took revenge by winning a close foul-ridden game on their home floor in Game 3, the Nuggets destroyed the Hornets in Game 4, playing with a balanced offensive output coupled with the most perfect defense any team could ever play. They limited the Hornets to just 63 points while winning the game with almost just as much of a cushion of an all-time playoff high deficit of 58 points. Though it was a balanced effort on offense, Melo led the Nuggets with an efficient 26-point output.

It seemed that the Nuggets were doing well, and after losing in five straight playoff appearances, Anthony and the Nuggets finally won their first playoff series since 1994 by beating the disheartened and discouraged New Orleans Hornets on their home floor by 21 points. Anthony scored 34 points, and it was also his first-ever playoff series win. In the post-game interview, Melo said that it was a complete relief to have had the load taken off after five years of not being able to win a playoff series. It was because Carmelo Anthony was finally going to the second round for the first time in his NBA career.

In their next playoff series, the Nuggets faced a Dallas Mavericks team that was also playing on a high after defeating perennial championship contenders, the San Antonio Spurs. Having home-court advantage to open the series helped Denver quickly, and they rallied from a first-quarter deficit to end the game with a 14-point victory. While Anthony took only ten shots, he still finished the game with 23 points. The star of the opening match was Nene, who scored 24 points on only 13 shot attempts. Melo and Nene were once again the stars in Game 2 as they each had 25 points while Smith had 21 off the bench on the way to a 117-105 win over the Mavs to get a 2-0 lead.

Game 3 in Dallas was even tighter and more physical. Neither team gave an edge in a game in where more than 60 fouls were called. When the game was ready for the Mavs' taking as they had a one-point lead in the dying seconds, Carmelo Anthony was guarded closely by Antoine Wright, who was attempting to foul Melo to prevent a game-winning three-pointer. But with no bailing foul called, Carmelo Anthony got the space he needed to rise and make the game-winning three-point shot with merely a second left in the game. The Mavs could not convert, and the Nuggets had an insurmountable 3-0 lead in the series. The Mavs stayed alive for at least one more game as Dirk Nowitzki scored 44 points to combat the 41 of Melo in Game 5.

With the Western Conference Finals in their sights and the taste of victory only growing stronger, the Nuggets ran roughshod over the Dallas Mavericks in just five games in the conference semi-finals. In the closeout game, Anthony had a solid performance, scoring 30 points. The hard work was finally paying off. Denver advanced to the Conference Finals, but to their dismay, ran up against the Los Angeles Lakers squad led by Kobe Bryant and legendary head coach Phil Jackson. The Lakers had swept them the previous season in the first round, and they were better equipped for a title run, especially with Kobe Bryant leading a pair of 7-foot giants on the Laker frontline.

However, the Nuggets were a lot different from the team the Lakers swept just a year before. Iverson was not around anymore, and neither was Marcus Camby. Nevertheless, the

2008-09 Denver Nuggets were just as potent on the offensive end while maintaining a serviceable defensive scheme on the other part of the court. Best of all, Billups had more chemistry with Anthony than Allen Iverson ever had.

This was also the second playoff meeting between Carmelo Anthony and Kobe Bryant, who share the same transcendent scoring mentality that past NBA greats have had. While Anthony had always looked up to Kobe ever since he saw the Mamba play opposite Michael Jordan in the 1998 All-Star Game in New York, Bryant had treated Anthony as a rival until they became close in the 2008 Beijing Olympics.

Just before the season began, Carmelo Anthony joined a star-studded cast of NBA greats in their prime years in the Beijing Olympic Games to represent the United States of America. One of those superstars was Kobe Bryant, who was one of the headliners of that team along with LeBron James. It was then that the two prolific scorers realized that they had a lot more in common than they initially thought.

While LeBron James was out there organizing team meals to acquaint the Team USA athletes with each other, Kobe Bryant was often found alone, looking focused like the Black Mamba he was, seemingly meditating on how to beat his opponents. It was the same scenario during practices. With so much talent on that roster, the only other person on that team that could match up to Bryant's focused mentality towards the game of basketball was Carmelo Anthony.

Because of their similar disposition towards basketball, Carmelo Anthony and Kobe Bryant suddenly became the best of friends on that Team USA squad. Both superstars came into the NBA the same way as aloof young teenagers looking to rise to become a part of the league's elite. Aside from that, both players have also experienced more or less the same type of off-court issues only to move past those and take their respective games to new heights.

Bonding with Kobe in Beijing also helped Carmelo improved as a player. Bryant would often joke about how Anthony stole his pull-up jumper.[viii] It seemed as if the joke was real; Melo suddenly became more adept in that department. Nevertheless, that was part of what made Carmelo Anthony an even more exceptional player than he already was. Melo would treat Kobe like a big brother from then on.

But the Conference Finals were a different story as the two close friends faced off on opposite ends. Despite a seemingly Cinderella season waiting in the fold, the Lakers outplayed the

Nuggets in the Conference Finals. Game 1 was close, and the two superstars battled it out for supremacy. Melo had 39 points while Kobe had 40. In the end, Kobe's team triumphed with a 2-point win. Game 2 was an encore for the two superstars. Anthony scored 34 while Bryant had 32. But this time, it was the Nuggets who eked out a close three-point victory to tie the series at one win apiece.

Kobe Bryant continued his scoring rampage in Game 3 as the series shifted over to Denver. The legendary player scored 41 points to get the victory on the Nuggets' home floor. Meanwhile, Melo only had 21 in that game. In a complete team effort in Game 4, the Nuggets blew the Lakers out, 120 to 101, to tie the series once again. However, the Lakers rallied, and the Nuggets never came close to winning the series.

In what was supposed to be another shootout between the two superstar scorers, Kobe Bryant instead became the bait as he only attempted 13 shots for 22 points compared to the 31 of Carmelo. The strategy paid off as the Lakers won the game, 103 to 94. With the Nuggets reeling and one loss away from the end of their dream season, they were intent on forcing a Game 7.

Unfortunately, the LA Lakers were just too experienced and well-coached to lose the close-out game. Kobe Bryant continued his torrid scoring pace with 35 points while Carmelo Anthony only had 25 as he dropped a matchup between two incredible scorers as well as the Western Conference Finals. Melo and the Nuggets' dream season was over, but their future seemed bright, as there was a lot of chemistry between Anthony and Billups. Carmelo Anthony averaged a then career-best 27.2 points along with 5.8 rebounds and 4.1 assists in 16 playoff games that season.

After losing to the Lakers in the Western Conference Finals, the Denver Nuggets had no reason to be disappointed, especially after defying expectations and reaching farther than any Nuggets team had ever gone before. They were only going to get better primarily because of the chemistry between their two best players.

At the start of the 2009-10 season, Carmelo Anthony showed no signs of offseason rust. With only two games into the new regular season, he already scored a total of 71 points. In their season and home opener, Melo scored 30. He followed up that performance with a 41-point explosion against Portland.

The third game provided the opportunity for Anthony to impress fans and naysayers. This time, he scored 42 points. He had a total of 113 points in just the first three games of the season. And for the first time in over two decades, the Denver Nuggets were unbeaten in the first three games. Because of that, Anthony was named the NBA Player of the Week and Western Conference Player of the Month.

Early in the season, Carmelo Anthony was already making a good run for the scoring championship since he was leading the league in scoring with 30.2 points. Because of that, he was also figured early into the MVP conversation. He never scored below 20 points in the first 15 games of the season. It did not take Anthony a long time to further stake his claim as one of the best scorers in the league when he upped his career-high to 50 points versus the New York Knicks. Chauncey Billups added 32 points to the board that night, making them only the third pair of players in league history to score 50 and 30 in one game.

That 50-point game against the New York Knicks would turn out to be a preview of things to come for Carmelo and New York. Anthony had long wanted to play for the Knicks because he grew up watching the team. That performance on November 27, 2009, was his unofficial audition for the New York Knicks.

Proving that he was arguably the best scorer in the NBA that season, Carmelo Anthony would turn over a few more high-scoring outputs as the season went on. Early in December, Melo had a five-game stretch wherein he did not score below 30 points. That included a 40-point outburst in a narrow loss to the Detroit Pistons. He would end that barrage with 38 points in a win over the Houston Rockets. Two games later, he would score 41 against the Grizzlies.

In January 2010, Anthony's popularity was felt when he was named as a starter for the 2010 NBA All-Star Game for the second time in his young professional career. That All-Star Game start was Carmelo Anthony's third overall midseason classic selection. It was a bounce-back season for Melo, who had not been an All-Star the previous year. Carmelo Anthony made his name known by leading the Western Conference All-Stars in scoring. He had a double-double performance with 27 points and ten boards.

After the All-Star break, the Nuggets went on to face the Cleveland Cavaliers, who were unbeaten in 13 straight games. LeBron had a better individual performance and recorded a triple-double night. He finished the game with 43 points, 13 boards, and 15 dimes. On the other hand, Melo had a similar outing when he posted 40 points, six rebounds, and seven assists. In the usual Anthony fashion, he nailed a jumper with just 1.9 seconds left in the game as James' efforts to defend him went in vain. With that, the Cavaliers' streak ended, and

Carmelo Anthony proved to the world that he was not merely a scoring machine, but also one of the most clutch NBA players on the planet. That was not his lone game-winner because he also nailed one on the Toronto Raptors late in March of that year.

The Denver Nuggets finished the season with a record of 53-29. Anthony averaged 28.2 points, 6.6 rebounds, and 3.2 assists. After starting the season as the highest scoring player, he eventually slowed down and lost the scoring championship race to Kevin Durant of the Oklahoma City Thunder. Nevertheless, Melo's ability to score points in bunches earned him a reputation for being one of the deadliest scorers in the league. He had seven total games of scoring at least 40 points that season.

The Nuggets were off to face a Utah Jazz team that featured the deadly pick-and-roll combo of Deron Williams and Carlos Boozer. The series was a face-off between the fourth and fifth seeds, and it shaped up to be the tightest playoff series in the West that season. Carmelo Anthony also had to get his team back on track in a tough Western Conference setting.

The Nuggets immediately gave the fight to the Jazz in the opening game, courtesy of another incredible performance by

Carmelo Anthony. Melo had a then-career playoff high of 42 points as Denver went on to win the game by 13 points. He was practically unstoppable in Game 1 when he seemed like he could not miss from the floor. Carmelo Anthony shot 18 out of 25 in that game. Naturally, his teammates kept feeding him.

Melo followed up that great game with a 32-point output in Game 2. But Deron Williams matched his output with 33 points as the Jazz escaped with a tight three-point win. However, Anthony was less efficient in that game. He shot 9 out of 25 from the floor in that outing but was the recipient of hard fouls. Melo made 14 of his 15 free throw attempts that game.

In Utah, Deron Williams once again broke the hearts of Nuggets fans as he scored 24 points and assisted on ten baskets to fend off the Denver-based team led by 25 each from Anthony and Billups. Though Melo shot better for Denver in that game, his 25-point effort was not enough to take a win in Utah.

Losing in Game 2 proved to be consequential for the Denver Nuggets because the Jazz held on to both of their first two home games. Melo's 39 was for naught as the Jazz went on to win Game 4 by 11 points. Down 1-3 in the series, Melo willed the Nuggets back into contention with a double-double performance when he scored 26 points and grabbed 11 rebounds to close the gap to 2-3.

Carmelo Anthony posted another double-double performance with 20 points and 12 rebounds in Game 6. However, the Jazz held on to win the game to the roar of their home crowd, 104 to 112. So after a dream season in the 2009 playoffs, the Nuggets were out of contention early in the first round of 2010. Though their core stayed the same, their problem during the 2010 playoffs was their defense. They struggled to contain the Utah Jazz team that averaged more than 110 points per game in their series. Their star player was still playing like a top-five player in the league, but unfortunately, his lack of playoff success might have rendered him unhappy with the Denver Nuggets.

Final Days in Denver, the Trade to the Knicks

Before the 2010-11 season, Carmelo Anthony refused to sign a proposed contract extension offered by the Nuggets. The Denver Nuggets were willing to sign their superstar to a $65 million contract for a span of three seasons. However, he still declined the offer as reports came in that Anthony wanted to play elsewhere in the coming seasons.

Everyone knew that Anthony was from the East Coast, so rumors ran rampant that it was his dream destination—

specifically, New York, his birthplace. Further fueling the stories was the Manhattan location of his summer wedding. With that, reports came in that the All-Star forward had requested a trade to get out of the Denver Nuggets.

Kind wishes from friends and colleagues hinted at the young superstar trading in the laid-back mountain life for a faster-paced city life. Several other teams were interested, such as the Houston Rockets and New Jersey Nets. For Anthony's part, he wanted to play in a big market. Anthony's trade request was not fulfilled, and he began the season in a powder blue and yellow uniform on the Nuggets' court.

Despite his decision to stay in Denver, the next few months was uncomfortable for both him and the team. Everybody knew that he was on his way out. Questions about where he might end up at the end of the season were all around. It was all too obvious that he wanted out of Denver because he had refused to sign the dotted line on the franchise's extension offer.

Despite the many trade offers and suitors for the services of arguably the most complete scorer in the NBA at that time, it was inevitable that Carmelo Anthony would end up where he always wanted to play. He had always dreamed of playing for the New York Knicks ever since he was a little boy. He wanted to play under the bright lights of Madison Square Garden as New York hopefuls cheered him on, much like how he had cheered on Michael Jordan and Kobe Bryant when they squared off in the 1998 All-Star Game in the Big Apple. That was always his dream.

But to his merit, Anthony remained professional and composed throughout the trade drama. He still played his usual way, and he even notched a 20-20 game against the Phoenix Suns. He had 20 points and 22 rebounds. Melo also continued doing what he did best—hitting game-winning jumpers, such as the last-second shot against the Bulls in November.

Despite an excellent start to his season, Anthony was saddened by the loss of his sister Michelle. He learned of the death while in San Antonio with the team. Anthony immediately returned to Baltimore to support his family and missed five games, including a Christmas Day thriller.

Things would not go well for Anthony and the Nuggets as the season went on. Carmelo Anthony was always open in publicizing where he wanted to play. He wanted to be in New York. Because of that, other contending teams were hesitant to pitch in legitimate offers for the services of Anthony because they were so afraid of the prospect of Melo suddenly bolting in free agency to sign a contract with the Knicks.[ix]

Because of the "Melodrama," the Denver Nuggets were left constrained concerning their options. They had a once-in-a-lifetime superstar who did not want to stay with them anymore. Moreover, other teams were hesitant in offering deals that would have helped the Nuggets rebuild out of fear that Anthony might not sign an extension with them. With of all that, the Denver Nuggets suddenly started to stumble at the height of all the Melodrama.

Despite the fact that Carmelo Anthony was in the middle of all the negotiations and drama surrounding the Nuggets, the superstar forward's focus was still towards playing basketball at the highest level. When it seemed like his stay in Denver was down to its final days, Melo had 50 points and 11 rebounds in a loss to the Houston Rockets on February 7. Three days later, he scored 42 in a win over Dallas. His final game as a Nugget was a 38-point outburst in Milwaukee, and it seemed evident that he was intent on going to New York.

But Nuggets General Manager Masai Ujiri was not going to be held ransom by Carmelo Anthony. Though he had already succumbed to the thought that Melo would only want to be traded to New York, he still bargained for the highest possible price he could get for Anthony. He negotiated hard with the New York Knicks management, who were also hesitant about giving up some of their key players.[ix]

Gambling on the chances of Denver landing vital young players in the trade, Ujiri started shopping elsewhere in New York's neighboring state of New Jersey. The New Jersey Nets were rumored to someday relocate to Brooklyn, New York. Though the Nets were not the Knicks, Melo's dream of playing in New York would still come to fruition.[ix]

Out of fear that Carmelo Anthony would end up on their rival's roster, the Knicks pulled out all the stops to acquire the superstar forward. What began as conversations and offers made by general managers turned into negotiations between franchise owners. That was the move that Ujiri had anticipated the Knicks would make.[ix]

The Anthony trade saga finally ended on February 22, 2011, with a blockbuster three-team trade. Many teams had courted the All-Star forward, including the New Jersey Nets, Cleveland Cavaliers, Los Angeles Clippers, and Toronto Raptors. In the end, New York came out victorious thanks to the Denver

Nuggets' efforts in trying to get the highest possible price for their superstar.

Anthony was sent together with Billups to the New York Knicks. In exchange, the Denver Nuggets received a package of excellent players like Wilson Chandler, Raymond Felton, and Danilo Gallinari, together with role-playing 7-footers Timofey Mozgov and Kosta Koufos. Reportedly, Anthony signed a three-year extension worth $65 million with the Knicks. He was now a member of the New York Knicks and bid farewell to the Denver Nuggets, the team that had drafted him and made him their franchise player for 8½ years. He was averaging 25.2 points and 7.6 rebounds in 50 games with the Nuggets before the trade.

The trade to the New York Knicks was a dream that finally came true for Carmelo Anthony, who had always set his eyes on playing in the Big Apple someday. The Knicks were his favorite team, and the mindset for him ever since he saw Michael Jordan and Kobe Bryant under the bright lights of Madison Square Garden in 1998 was that he was going to be in New York as a superstar someday.

When introduced to the media by Knicks owner James Dolan, Carmelo Anthony was still in disbelief that his childhood dream had finally come true. His thought was that he was just a visiting player in hostile territory. Melo felt like he was a Nugget trying to break the hearts of the New York hopefuls. Nevertheless, he was overjoyed to be there finally. The Melodrama was over, and Carmelo Anthony was going to be in full focus from then on.[x] With the Knicks, Anthony chose to wear the number 7 instead because New York had already retired his number 15 jersey. He was joining a struggling Knicks franchise that was hoping to go back to their glory days as one of the best teams in the NBA. Fortunately, the Knicks seemed as if they were on track as Melo was on for a ship that included athletic power forward Amar'e Stoudemire, fresh from the Phoenix Suns a season ago, and offensive head coach Mike D'Antoni. Stoudemire was second in the league in scoring before the trade. Meanwhile, D'Antoni was notorious for his fast-paced, high-scoring style of coaching. Anthony teaming up with Stoudemire gave the Knicks a deadly duo of forwards and possibly the highest-scoring frontline in the NBA.

In his first game with New York, Carmelo scored 27 points with ten rebounds in a win versus the Bucks. It was at that moment— his first game with New York— when Carmelo Anthony made the Knicks his team. Though he was playing in an unfamiliar system, Melo never seemed bothered by it at all. His focus was on basketball, and his clutch baskets in the final stretch of the game were what sealed the win for the Knicks. For Anthony, that debut for the New York Knicks was also how he got all the stress of the Melodrama out of his system. He was finally able to focus on what he loved to do the most on the team he loved more than any other.[xi]

Carmelo Anthony would score at least 20 points in the next five games as he added a much-needed superstar to complement the high-scoring front line of the New York Knicks, who were used to relying merely on Stoudemire before the Melo trade. The injection of Anthony into the lineup invigorated New York's chances at a playoff spot despite being notoriously known over the past few seasons as a fodder team in the East.

Melo averaged 26.3 points and 6.7 rebounds in 27 games with the Knicks. He averaged 25.6 points and 7.3 rebounds for the whole season. The deal to get Anthony proved to be advantageous as the Knicks were able to power for the sixth spot in the Eastern Conference, where they went on to face the Boston Celtics. During the series, the Knicks were as hobbled as any team could ever be. Amar'e Stoudemire and Chauncey Billups were both out with injuries. In Game 2, Carmelo Anthony exploded for 42 points together with 17 rebounds, but it was an effort in vain since the Knicks lost that one. In the end, the injuries proved to be detrimental for the Knicks, and they were swept in the first round of the playoffs.

Playing in the Big Apple

Having Anthony in the lineup meant that the New York Knicks were headed in a new direction and were intent on building on their two scoring forwards. To complement the scoring abilities of Melo and Amar'e, they decided to bring in Tyson Chandler via a sign-and-trade deal to anchor the Knicks' defense. The problem was that they did not have enough salary cap space to shoulder Chandler's contract. This forced the Knicks front office to use their one-time amnesty clause on Chauncey Billups, effectively waiving his contract. Without a point guard to run Mike D'Antoni's high-octane offense, the Knicks decided to sign Mike Bibby to a veteran's minimum, hoping he could bring balance to the attack.

The Knicks were full of optimism entering the 2011-12 season since they had Carmelo Anthony playing with them for a whole season for the first time. However, the Knicks could not get enough traction at the start of the lockout-shortened 66-game season. Experts noted that Coach Mike D'Antoni's, "Get it done now!" and, "Seven seconds or less" offense approaches were a stark contrast to Anthony's isolation style of play. Moreover,

Carmelo was sidelined with an injury that forced him to miss 11 games.

That 11-game stretch turned out to be a gift for the Knicks. Mike Bibby was a bust as the starting point guard, and they were forced to start the rookie shooting guard Iman Shumpert as their playmaker. Shumpert was the next to be bitten by the injury bug, and D'Antoni was forced to thrust third-string point guard Jeremy Lin into the starting role. Lin made his coach look like a genius. The point guard from Harvard carried the Knicks' offense throughout Anthony's absence, scoring at a high pace and facilitating the offense the way D'Antoni wanted all his point guards to do. The point guard guided his team to a seven-game win streak even without Anthony and Stoudemire, and the Knicks climbed back up to .500. That short stretch of success was dubbed as the "Linsanity" period.

Anthony came back from injury, and the Knicks fans were optimistic about the possibility of their team playing at a season high, especially with the Linsanity phenomenon complementing the scoring abilities of Carmelo Anthony and free agent acquisition JR Smith. But it turned out otherwise. Melo's ball-dominating style could not gel well with the facilitating prowess and point guard-centric offense that Mike D'Antoni wanted to run. On top of that, Jeremy Lin thrived in breaking down offenses with his ability to slash into the lane. That style did not gel well with Carmelo's preferred offensive attack.

Even with Melo back in the lineup, the Knicks went back to their losing ways, dropping seven of their next eight games. The pressures of handling a superstar lineup and the scrutiny coming from such a big market led D'Antoni to step down as head coach of the New York Knicks. His assistant Mike Woodson took over and instilled a defensive attitude that had the Knicks winning 18 out of the next 24 games to qualify for a playoff spot.

Mike Woodson's defensive philosophy gave new life to the struggling Knicks, who had to brace the entire season due to the injuries that Melo and Amar'e had suffered. For Melo's part, playing for a coach that trusted his ability score made him an even better player near the tail end of the regular season. In April alone, Carmelo Anthony had two 40-point outputs while also figuring himself above 30 points per game for most of the time. He even had triple-double production on April 17, 2013, when he finished a win over Boston with 35 points, 12 rebounds, and ten assists.

Despite all of the drama and injuries, Carmelo Anthony was an All-Star and a member of the All-NBA Third Team by averaging 22.6 points, 6.7 rebounds, and 3.6 assists while shooting barely 44% from the floor. The injuries, struggles with teammates, and coaching changes all contributed to what was a subpar season for Carmelo Anthony, who is believed to be more than what he showed that season.

The Knicks went into the playoffs as the seventh seed in the Eastern Conference. They went on to match up against the powerhouse Miami Heat team. What seemed unusual about the matchup was that Melo was headed to face off the Big Three of the Miami Heat composed of LeBron James, Dwyane Wade, and Chris Bosh. What is even more interesting about that was that those three players were draft mates of Anthony's back in the 2003 NBA Draft, and it was indeed a date with destiny, as four of the top five draftees of that year would meet nine years later in a battle for Eastern supremacy. The problem was that the other three players were playing on the same team while Melo was a lone star in New York.

To be a formidable opponent, Anthony needed to give up some of the more questionable shots in his arsenal. The long-two and the dribble-up-three were not successful in improving the team's overall record. Anthony possessed strength and swiftness that would better be used in calling for the ball at the post and getting the better of his man. His assists were not always impressive, but there was no denying his passing talent. Anthony received considerable attention from opposing defenses but was not regularly willing to give up the ball to someone with a quality look at the basket.

Meanwhile, the Knicks continued to be jinxed with injuries. Several key players could not stay healthy. Chandler was not in the best form because of the flu that had kept him out of Game 1. They were missing the services of Iman Shumpert, who had shown to be a capable defensive gem, because of a season-ending injury he suffered. Moreover, the only other productive player, Amar'e Stoudemire, was struggling to get back to his All-Star form throughout that year.

Not even Jeremy Lin, who suffered an injury right when the regular season was about to end, could save the Knicks from the impending doom that the Miami Heat were about to befall on them. Every burden was placed on the shoulders of Carmelo Anthony who, for all his talents and prowess, was still a lone man against an army of All-Stars in their respective prime years.

Nevertheless, Carmelo Anthony was responsible for the end of the New York Knicks' playoff win drought. When the Knicks were down 0-3 in the series, and when it was elementary that they were going to be eliminated, Melo made a point not to go quietly into the night. He was practically unstoppable in Game 4 on his way to 41 points on 15 out of 29 shooting from the floor. Because of that performance, Anthony gave New York the franchise's first playoff win in a span of as much as ten seasons. Though everyone knew that the series was done, that win gave hope to the Knicks' fan base.

Scoring Champion Season

In the ensuing offseason, the New York Knicks were intent on bolstering their lineup for a possible run at an NBA title now that no more distractions were plaguing the team. Although they lost their starting point guard Jeremy Lin to the Houston Rockets via free agency, the addition of veteran point guards Jason Kidd and Raymond Felton more than made up for the loss of Linsanity. Among other veterans they acquired were Kurt Thomas, Marcus Camby, and Pablo Prigioni from Argentina. The powerhouse lineup also enticed veteran big man Rasheed Wallace to come out of retirement in the hopes of winning another NBA title.

Carmelo Anthony only became better in the offseason after being one of the veteran leaders in a star-studded yet young Team USA in the 2012 London Olympics. Working with some of the best talents in the world proved to help Melo in many ways during that gold medal run. Not only was he one of the top scorers on the team, but he was also one of the critical voices in that locker room.

He even earned the praise of Patrick Ewing, one of the many NBA legends that have donned a New York Knicks jersey. A former Olympian himself, Ewing saw how Carmelo Anthony had matured in his stint with the Olympic team in 2012. He said that his experience in Team USA made him a better leader.[xii] Ewing saw the same thing in Melo. The superstar forward was already strapped in for what would become arguably his best season as a pro.

The start of the 2012-2013 season saw Carmelo Anthony becoming a legitimate MVP contender. Arguably one of the best pure scorers on the planet, Anthony remained a fearless assassin, killing countless teams with big shots during his career, including his time with the Knicks. He was not only scoring in bunches, but he was also contributing in many ways to get his team to victories. Melo was rebounding, assisting, and stealing at a pace unseen from him in past seasons. His impressive start led many people to believe that he was likely to become the MVP of that season.

There were many 40-point games, but the Knicks remained marginal, at best, and the dualism of Anthony being both a selfish and selfless player became the topic of many sports commentators and fans. He was determined to disprove the headlines and grumblings that he was a ball-hog who quit on his coach, did not play defense, and was out of shape. Anthony wanted to change the perception.

On the court, though, Anthony's shooting performance continued to sizzle. He set the Knicks' franchise record with 31 straight games of scoring 20 or more points. The previous record was 20 consecutive games. His best performance at that time was his 50-point outburst versus the Big Three of the championship Miami Heat.

What was unusual in that performance was that Carmelo Anthony did all of his damage from the perimeter. He did not score a single basket in the painted area. In the next game after putting up 40 against the Hawks in a win, he lit the Milwaukee Bucks up for 41. With those performances, Carmelo Anthony became the only other player in New York franchise history since Bernard King to score at least 40 points in three straight games.

Melo was practically unstoppable that season as he tore open the NBA with his ability to score and newfound maturity on the leadership end. With Carmelo Anthony leading the way, the Knicks won their division title for the first time in almost two decades. Playing in New York as a superstar also benefited the popularity of Carmelo Anthony. Melo was one of the top-selling players concerning merchandise in the whole NBA.

In that loss, Anthony had 36 points and 19 incredible rebounds. With that performance, he once again rewrote the record books for the Knicks when he set a team record six straight games of 35 or more points. Impressively, Anthony sat out the entire fourth quarter in an easy win over the Cleveland Cavaliers, but still had an outstanding, dominant performance of 31 points and 14 rebounds. Kevin Durant's decision to sit out his last regular season game against the Milwaukee Bucks proved to be advantageous for Anthony as he barely secured his first-ever scoring championship. He averaged an NBA-high 28.7 points to go along with 6.9 rebounds and 2.6 assists.

It was a fantastic season for Carmelo Anthony, who piled up the scoring numbers and was an All-Star and a member of the All-NBA Second Team. His scoring numbers impressed former naysayers. Under the tutelage of defensive coach Mike Woodson, Melo improved defensively. No longer was he sleeping on his defensive assignments. He kept a close eye on what the opposing offense was doing throughout the game. He also made good use of his athletic ability and wingspan to cover opposing players and make life miserable for them.

Carmelo Anthony also grew to be a strong leader that season, as veteran leaders like Jason Kidd and Tyson Chandler groomed him for that role. His leadership had the Knicks winning game after game even as Amar'e Stoudemire was struggling to get back to All-Star form that year because of all the injuries he had suffered.

JR Smith also proved to be an excellent second option for the Knicks, even coming off the bench. There was always something about Smith that made him better when playing behind Carmelo Anthony. For JR's efforts the entire year, he was given the Sixth Man of the Year award. Raymond Felton also enjoyed a resurgent season after struggling in Denver and Portland. Reigning Defensive Player of the Year Tyson Chandler was also an All-Star that season for anchoring the Knicks defense. Everything was going well for the Knicks, and they were on their way to do some severe damage in the playoffs as the second seed in the Eastern Conference.

During the first round of 2013 NBA Playoffs, the New York Knicks defeated the Boston Celtics in six games. He had 21 points in the closeout game. It was not his best game against the aging core of the Celtics, however, as he scored 36 and 34 in Games 1 and 2 victories. He then had 36 in an overtime loss in Game 4. The Knicks had not won a first playoff series since the days when Patrick Ewing was looming inside the Madison Square Garden paint. New York hopefuls were happy to see their team going back to their winning ways. In that series, Anthony upped his play as he averaged 29.2 points.

However, the celebrations were short-lived. Although it took six games, the Indiana Pacers eventually defeated the Knicks. Going up against the defense of Paul George had Melo struggling, but he did his best to do what he does better than anyone—score baskets. He scored 35 points as the Knicks won Game 2 on their home floor. He was limited to merely a little over 20 points in four of the first five games of the series but then exploded for 39 in Game 6.

His effort was not enough as the Pacers went on to eliminate them in that match. Carmelo Anthony and the Knicks seemed as if they had found their traction to stay as a powerhouse in the Eastern Conference though they had lost in a fierce effort in the second round. Fans thought so as well. Unfortunately, things would not go as planned.

Back to Earth, Rebuilding Era

After an excellent 2012-13 season, the Knicks were headed in a new direction in 2013-14. Unfortunately, the path was down. Starting point guard and veteran leader Jason Kidd retired in the offseason to end an incredible Hall of Fame career. The team also traded a few of their veteran pieces to bring in Andrea Bargnani. After his phenomenal season as a sixth man, JR Smith's contract was renewed for another three years. Among other additions were Metta World Peace (formerly Ron Artest) and capable rookie shooter Tim Hardaway Jr. Although the Knicks would lose only a few key pieces, they were not able to replicate the season they had the previous year.

The Knicks' start to the 2013–2014 NBA season was dismal. They suffered a nine-game losing streak and were quickly down to a 3-13 win-loss record. Nevertheless, in what had become customary, Anthony continued to play his best as the Knicks continued to lose. He averaged 26.3 points, 9.9 rebounds, and 1.1 steals through the first 16 games. He also had nine double-doubles in that stretch.

Despite the horrible start to the season, Carmelo Anthony tried to right the direction of the ship with his incredible scoring abilities. The Knicks went up 4-1 at the onset of 2014 as they piled up big wins against the likes of the Miami Heat and the Spurs. His efforts did not go unheralded as he won the Eastern Conference Player of the Week award.

On January 24, 2014, Carmelo Anthony capped off an incredible start to the year by establishing a new career high and breaking the single-game record for most points in Madison Square Garden. Melo broke the record of his close friend Kobe Bryant, who once scored 61 points in MSG by scoring 62 points and grabbing 13 rebounds.

That performance was the pinnacle of Carmelo Anthony's scoring prowess. It was the culmination of what he had always dreamed of as a kid—dazzling the New York City crowd with his excellent abilities. There was nothing that the Charlotte Bobcats could do against him in that game. Melo's shot chart was green at all angles on the floor. He shot 23 out of 35 from the floor, 6 out of 11 from the three-point line, and 10 out of 10 from the foul stripe for those 62 points in only a little over 38 minutes of action. That record still stands as the best single-game effort in the Mecca of basketball.

Despite having one of the more memorable performances of the season, Carmelo Anthony was still struggling to boost the morale of his New York Knicks. If anything, his 62-point game was just a consolation prize for what was otherwise a disappointment. The superstar from Baltimore was probably the only relevant thing about the Knicks that year.

Though the Knicks played horribly, Carmelo Anthony was still voted as a starter in his seventh career All-Star Game. Melo continued his torrid scoring rate even as he played with and against the brightest stars of the game. He scored 30 points, which included an All-Star record eight 3-point shots. He teamed up with 2014 NBA All-Star Game MVP Kyrie Irving of the Cleveland Cavaliers, who scored a game-high of 31 points. Their collaboration helped the Eastern Conference team erase a 13-point half-time deficit and snap a three-game losing streak to their Western Conference counterparts with a 163-155 victory. Aside from the 3-point record, Anthony was also part of yet another All-Star record as the teams combined for a total of 318 points to surpass the 303 total points in 1987.

Carmelo was not done after a fantastic performance in the All-Star Game. In a span of just four games from February 19 up to 24, Melo had a combined output of 165 points, which included three games of scoring at least 40. Nevertheless, the Knicks were still horrible even as their leader was technically doing it all. They were 1-3 in that stretch where Anthony had to carry the entire load.

Anthony wrapped up the 2013-2014 season averaging 27.4 points, 8.1 rebounds, and 3.1 assists in a league-leading 38.7 minutes per game. However, even with those numbers, he missed the NBA playoffs for the first time in his career. Carmelo Anthony suffered a double black eye of sorts when the Knicks finished the season at 37-45, a 17-game-win decline from the previous season, which fulfilled what ESPN predicted via Kevin Pelton's computerized SCHOENE projection system.

Before the season started, Anthony was critical of the computer's prediction, saying that machines are prone to glitches and that he did not believe in predictions. However, when the 2013-2014 season was over, ESPN's insider prediction was correct in saying that the drop in three-point accuracy, as a result of the departure of Jason Kidd, Steve Novak, and Chris Copeland, would be the Knicks' downfall. Accurate enough, the lack of floor-spacers enabled the defense to clamp down on Carmelo, limiting his shots. The injuries suffered by their key frontline players and their poor start to the season was a premonition that would lead to the downfall of Mike Woodson in the Big Apple.

Woodson led the Knicks to a record of 109-79 in three seasons, which included playoff appearances in his first two seasons. But after missing the playoffs during Phil Jackson's arrival as Knicks President, Woodson's head was the first one put on the chopping block.

Enter Phil Jackson and Derek Fisher, Anchor of the Triangle

There were rumors that Phil Jackson would soon take over as head coach while running the team as its President, similar to how Pat Riley did when he first came to the Miami Heat. But even while the power struggle for the head coaching job was only starting to escalate, Carmelo Anthony was vocal about his support for Mike Woodson. Anthony also went on to say, on record, that he would give Woodson his "recommendation" to stay in New York. However, a few days after Anthony said that, Jackson axed Woodson and the Knicks officially became a flock of sheep without a shepherd.

On June 10, 2014, the New York Knicks announced that they had hired former Los Angeles Lakers guard Derek Fisher as their new head coach. Fisher had won five NBA world championships with Jackson as coach in Los Angeles. More than his knack for hitting clutch three-point baskets, Fisher was an outstanding locker room guy. He had no coaching experience, but he had mastered the triangle offensive system in Los Angeles under the guidance of Jackson. Although Jackson did not mention implementing the triangle system in New York, the whole world was expecting the Knicks to run it when the 2015 season began.

Much talk about the triangle offense revolved around Carmelo Anthony. This is because when Jackson won his 11 NBA titles in Chicago and Los Angeles, he won all of them with one prominent scorer as the focal point of his offense. In Chicago, Jackson transformed Michael Jordan from a one-man scoring machine into a complete offensive weapon, and later into the greatest players in the history of basketball. In Los Angeles, he converted Kobe Bryant from a high-flying, slam-dunking teenager into the Black Mamba.

The same was expected of Carmelo Anthony in New York. Anthony always had the offensive skill set, but he had never had the right system to make it flourish. Offensively, Melo could have been just as talented as Jordan or Bryant. He also had the same venom running through his veins. However, something was always missing. Jackson's arrival as President and Fisher's hiring as head coach were seen as good omens for Madison

Square Garden. But before the Knicks got into that part of the equation, there was one big issue to settle: Carmelo Anthony.

Anthony had an opt-out clause in his existing contract, and many were speculating that he would exercise that right at the end of the season, especially after another year of failure at the team level. Phil Jackson tried to dissuade Anthony from opting out, but Anthony had his mind set on the July 1 free agency. On June 24, 2014, Carmelo Anthony opted out of the final year of his contract to test the free-agent market.

In his announcement, Anthony professed his love for New York, the Knicks, and their fans. But he also said that he wanted to explore other options at that stage of his career. Although Anthony forfeited his $23.33 million salary for the next season, he also opened the doors for a more lucrative long-term deal that would ensure his financial security. At the same time, exploring other offers could open up the possibility of moving to title contenders like LeBron James did in 2010 when he left Cleveland to play for Miami.

Anthony had many suitors, including contenders like Miami, Houston, Dallas, and Chicago. Even the skidding Los Angeles Lakers were serious in their bid to get the former Syracuse star on their team. However, on July 14, 2014, the New York

Knicks announced that they had re-signed Carmelo Anthony for a five-year deal worth $124 million.

Anthony's contract also had another player termination option after the fourth year and was unique because it also included a no-trade clause, which made Carmelo Anthony a New York Knick virtually for life, if he wanted to stay there, of course. With their franchise cornerstone secured, Phil Jackson continued to assemble the cast that would help Carmelo Anthony fulfill his promise.

On June 25, 2014, Phil Jackson completed his first trade as President of the New York Knicks. Jackson shipped out disgruntled center Tyson Chandler to the Dallas Mavericks in a six-player deal that also included troubled point guard Raymond Felton. In return, the Knicks received Spanish point guard Jose Calderon, veteran big man Samuel Dalembert, and two other reserves.

Chandler's trade was the first indication of Phil Jackson's willingness to overhaul the Knicks' roster to form a winning team around Anthony. But the Knicks' quest for a second superstar to pair with Anthony remained a dream because the Knicks still had the huge contracts of Amar'e Stoudemire and Andrea Bargnani on board until 2015.

Following the first trade that Jackson made with the Dallas Mavericks, Anthony believed that the team was headed in the right direction for rebuilding. Although he signed a maximum contract, Anthony said that he wanted the opportunity to win at this stage of his career more than the money. He added that he felt they had a brand new team with Phil Jackson and Derek Fisher at the helm and that he thought it was a new beginning that brought a whole new excitement out of him. However, Anthony probably spoke too soon.

The Knicks opened the 2014-2015 season on their home court against the Chicago Bulls. Ironically for Carmelo Anthony, the Bulls were one of his most preferred free agency destinations before his re-signing with the Knicks. The Bulls were composed of returning 2011 MVP Derrick Rose and new additions such as Pau Gasol, Aaron Brooks, rookie Doug McDermott, and Euro star Nikola Mirotić.

The raging Bulls apparently outmatched the Knicks, so they opened their 2014-2015 NBA regular season on the wrong foot. Carmelo Anthony led the Knicks with just 14 points on a disappointing 5-13 shooting from the field. The team looked lost on both ends of the floor, suffering on their defense rotations without Tyson Chandler and running an offense that resembled a flawed version of Jackson's vaunted triangle offensive system.

However, in their next game, the Knicks rebounded from that boo-filled blowout loss to the Bulls when they played against the highly touted Cleveland Cavaliers and the returning LeBron James. James struggled mightily in his first game in four years as a Cavalier at the Quicken Loans Arena, scoring just 17 points on 5-15 shooting from the floor and eight turnovers. In what was an emotional night in Cleveland, Carmelo Anthony took center stage and scored 25 points, including a baseline jump shot with LeBron James in his face that gave the Knicks a 92-87 lead with 25 seconds left to play. Anthony's clutch basket silenced the more than 20,000 fans that trooped to the Q to celebrate James' return to Cleveland. Likewise, it silenced the critics who had written off the Knicks after their ugly loss in their opening game against the Bulls.

In a 360-degree turnaround, that bounce-back game proved that if the Knicks could get their game going, they could compete against the best in the league. The question now was what kind of New York team would show up for the rest of the season.

Six games later, the Knicks were 2-6 and struggling under Phil Jackson. The Knicks had not scored 100 points in a match in eight games and were dead last in scoring with 91.1 points per game. Not only that, but the Knicks were also at the bottom of the league in free throw attempts and pace per game. For his part, Carmelo Anthony shot just 39% from the floor in the first eight games of the season and was averaging a career low of 5.3 rebounds through eight games played. The reason? Phil's Triangle offense.

The triangle system was easier read or said than done. Most of the time, the Knicks' offense looked like a square with Carmelo Anthony isolated on the other side and seemingly on an island by himself. Anthony was not getting any good looks from a stagnant offense and would often rush a weak shot with the shot clock winding down.

Anthony was not the only one trying to find his rhythm in the triangle. The rest of the Knicks were just as lost, and they spent more time thinking about what to do rather than just playing basketball. That mental preoccupation took its toll on the team, especially on the scorers, Anthony and J.R. Smith, who were used to creating strategies rather than passing the ball and moving it around.

Carmelo Anthony had slimmed down, much as LeBron James had, in a bid to play with more speed than power. But with his struggles, it looked as if Anthony was better off playing as an undersized power forward, creating mismatches on offense against the slower big men. But that had no place in the triangle system, which emphasizes movement, spacing, and passing. As a result, Anthony's scoring numbers went down along with his shooting percentages. Still, Phil Jackson believed that Anthony would soon adjust and flourish in the triangle offense like Jordan and Kobe did in the past. He urged the Knicks and their fans to be patient.

Eleven games later, the Knicks owned the third-worst record in the NBA at 4-15. They had lost 14 of their last 16 games and had been 3-14 since their win over the Cleveland Cavaliers during LeBron's first game back as a Cavalier. Little did they know that the Cavs would soon get their revenge.

The Knicks hosted the Cleveland Cavaliers for their 20th game of the season. Kyrie Irving took over with 37 points to lead the Cavs to a 90-87 win over the Knicks, who had now lost six games in a row. Carmelo Anthony epitomized their struggles, shooting a very ineffective 4-19 from the field and finishing with just 9 points.

With the loss, the Knicks tied the record for the worst start in franchise history at 4-16, which was established during their inaugural season in 1946-1947. On December 5, the 2014-15 New York Knicks broke that ignominious record with a loss to the Charlotte Hornets despite Carmelo Anthony scoring 32 points. The Knicks lost four more games in a row to get their first double-digit game-losing streak of the season at ten games. The Knicks then snapped their losing run at 10 with a December 12 win over the Boston Celtics where Carmelo Anthony was the top scorer with 22 points.

On December 16, the Knicks welcomed back Tyson Chandler and his Dallas Mavericks. The Mavs got off to a hot start by making 10 of their first 11 baskets, took a 12-point lead, and never looked back. Dallas beat New York to give the Knicks their worst start ever through 27 games at 5-22. For the first time, rookie coach Derek Fisher lashed out at his starters, including Carmelo Anthony, saying that they were a "disappointment" to their teammates.

Despite their struggles, Fisher had been cautious about not criticizing his players in public. But after this loss, it seemed that everything exploded in his face. Fisher had utilized 13 different starting lineups in 27 games, and not only were they struggling, but they also had vital people coming in and out because of injuries. For his part, Carmelo Anthony said that they had to believe that they could win games and not worry about losing.

On January 5, 2015, the Knicks traded former Sixth Man of the Year J.R. Smith and the injured Iman Shumpert to the Cleveland Cavaliers. In a deal that also involved the Oklahoma City Thunder, the Cavs parted with Dion Waiters to send him over to OKC. The Knicks got unheralded players in the form of seldom-used Lance Thomas, capable defender Lou Amundson, and a future second-round pick as compensation in the deal that seemed more of a cap space decision than an on-court need.

While the move was a good one financially, it did not improve the quality of players they had on their team. Essentially, the Knicks gave away two key players from their team and got nothing in return except a future second-rounder and cap flexibility going into the 2015 free agency. With the trade, Phil Jackson practically pulled the plug on the Knicks disaster season and put them on pace to become the worst team in NBA history. While the deal generated mixed reactions from New York fans, Carmelo Anthony still insisted that he trusted Phil's plans and that he firmly believed in his front-office decisions. However, the losing did not stop.

After twisting his knee on February 9, in a game against the Miami Heat, Anthony hinted that he was getting close to the point of shutting himself down for the rest of the season because his legs no longer had their usual bounce or pop. Still, there was no confirmation from the team that they would be doing that. Meanwhile, Anthony played through the pain and losses.

Despite growing concerns about his left knee, Carmelo Anthony was ready to play for the Eastern Conference team in the 2015 NBA All-Star Game. The theme for the 2015 NBA season had been injuries, and the 2015 midseason classic was not spared. Kobe Bryant, Blake Griffin, Dwyane Wade, and Anthony Davis were voted to the All-Star teams, but all begged off due to injuries. Had Anthony joined them, they would have tied 2007 and 1997 for the most All-Star Game injury replacements with five.

However, Anthony was determined to be the basketball ambassador of New York because the All-Star Game was to be held at the Barclay's Center. So despite the fact that he had missed the Knicks' game immediately before the All-Star break, he controversially "forced" his way into the match. Carmelo Anthony would play in the All-Star Game despite the injury. He would not have the best night of his life in that game. though he was kept open because of the traditional All-Star Game defense or the lack thereof.

On February 18, just after the All-Star Weekend, the New York Knicks announced that Carmelo Anthony would be undergoing a season-ending knee surgery. The procedure was to fix a torn left patella tendon. The injury had been plaguing him the last few games. It even held him to a bad performance during the All-Star Game, where the defense was at its most lax. With that surgery, the New York Knicks were high in hoping that Melo's game would return to the way it was mainly since they have him for a long-term period and on a lucrative contract that seemed impossible to trade away without his consent.

Anthony was already 30 years old and was already in his 12th NBA season, and the wear and tear of a hard-played career looked as if it was starting taking its toll on him. This was the most games he had missed in a single season since 2006-2007 when he missed 17 games in Denver. On the other hand, the Knicks had lost so many games that they were out of the playoff race at the All-Star break, so letting Anthony play through the pain to finish the season was more of a risk than shutting him down the rest of the way. The only unfinished business for the Knicks in the 2014-2015 season was whether they would get the #1 pick, and how bad their record would be. They were 10-30 with Anthony before the All-Star break, and there was little reason to believe they would do better without him with the kind of lineup that they had after Phil Jackson's player movements.

The Maturing Carmelo Anthony, Enter Porzingis

After a successful knee operation, Carmelo Anthony watched his Knicks break the wrong record and become the worst team in franchise history with a17-65 record. That bitter pill would have been easier to swallow had they gotten the worst record in the NBA, which would have given them the highest probability of landing the number 1 overall pick in the draft.

But alas, the short-handed Knicks won three of their last six games to finish one game better than the 16-66 Minnesota Timberwolves and squandered their opportunity to have their first number 1 overall pick since Patrick Ewing in 1985. As fate would have it, the Timberwolves ended up with the #1 pick and selected Kentucky's Karl-Anthony Towns. The Knicks picked fourth, and they took a leap of faith by unexpectedly drafting Latvia's seven-footer Kristaps Porzingis to the surprise of many basketball experts.

The Knicks' choice of Porzingis elicited boos from the crowd at the Barclays Center on draft night, but Carmelo Anthony gave him a high-tech welcome by congratulating and welcoming him to the team via text message. This was despite the fact that Melo had previously aired his thoughts about the pick. Though he was not degrading Porzingis' ability, he would have preferred if the Knicks had drafted someone ready to help him win instead of a long-term prospect such as the young Latvian. He would, however, learn to become close friends with the young Porzingis.

"The Zinger," as NBA TV analysts would later nickname him, turned out to become one of the biggest steals of the draft just as Carmelo Anthony had predicted after seeing firsthand what he could do during training camp. He came to the Knicks as one of many offseason acquisitions, including Robin Lopez, Derrick Williams, and Arron Afflalo, among others. But Porzingis stood—figuratively and literally, being 7'3"—above all of the new Knicks.

Kristaps Porzingis gave Anthony an excellent second option on offense. Many did not expect the 7'3" power forward to be so versatile on offense. He has the skills of a small forward and can shoot the ball like a shooting guard. Aside from his guard skills, Porzingis had a knack for finding offensive rebounds and flushing them down with an athletic ability unseen from a man his size. The boos that emanated from his draft night became cheers from the Madison Square faithful.

But even as the Zinger stole the limelight and hogged the highlight reel, Carmelo Anthony remained the focal point of the Knicks offense. Coming out of a season-ending injury is never easy, even for superstars of Melo's stature. However, he still led the Knicks in scoring with 21.3 points. He also upped his assists numbers as the focal point of the triangle offense with a career-high of 4.0 per game. The New York Knicks would still be on the losing end, but had improved from the season they had a year ago thanks to a healthier Melo and a steal of a draft pick in Porzingis. The fans voted Carmelo Anthony as a starter for the Eastern Conference All-Stars. It was his ninth overall appearance in the midseason classic and his seventh straight.

Carmelo Anthony resumed his duties as the glue guy for the New York Knicks as soon as the All-Star break was over. Though he was still a supreme scorer, Melo focused on trying to get his team better adjusted to the system that Phil Jackson wanted to implement in New York. Anthony could score 40 a night if he wanted to. He could carry the entire load repeatedly if he had a chance to do so. However, nearing the age of 32,

Carmelo Anthony was at the point of maturity where he would instead get his teammates involved.

Statistically, Anthony was in the middle of the worst season of long career even if he was still in the prime of his form. However, his mentality and maturity were at their highest points. Melo did not even bother to think that his rookie year was even better than his 2015-16 season. You could call it maturity or Jackson's influence, but Carmelo Anthony was happy with his place.

Out on the floor, you would still see Carmelo Anthony calling his shots and attempting difficult isolation plays. However, you would also see him doing other things that you rarely saw him do in the past. You would see him make crisp and Magic-esque passes that you never saw him do before. He would even grab more defensive rebounds than he ever did in his career instead of just running to the other end to attempt ill-advised fast break opportunities.[xiii]

The best part of all was that Carmelo Anthony seemed happier than ever. On and off the court, Melo was often smiling despite the fact that his Knicks were still nowhere near the level of competitiveness required even to make the postseason. Perhaps he has found his Zen moment and his inner peace after finally finding out, as Derek Fisher would say, that he could dominate the game in facets other than scoring.[xiii]

Carmelo Anthony was never the embodiment of a leader. But in a span of merely a season, everything seemed to change. He suddenly found it in himself to trust his teammates more despite the lack of talent on the roster. Porzingis, Calderon, Afflalo, and Williams were not the most talented group of players, but Anthony still found the courage in himself to try to incorporate his teammates into the offensive more than he ever did.

The old Carmelo Anthony would have forced his way into tough shots when doubled in the post or out on the perimeter. But the new version of the superstar forward made it a point to attract double teams so that he could hit his open teammates with crisp passes. His in-game attitude was not the only part that matured. Melo was also often seen playing cheerleader to Kristaps Porzingis, who was becoming one of the more popular players in New York. Despite the growing popularity of his young 7'3" teammate, there was no hint of jealousy in Carmelo Anthony the entire season as the once brash and cocky kid from Baltimore matured into the leader everyone thought he could be.[xiii]

Though his stats might not show it, and though the New York Knicks were facing another season without a playoff appearance having gone 32-50, it could be argued that Carmelo Anthony had one of the best seasons he has had in his career. And that is even though he averaged a low-scoring clip of 21.8 points to go along with 7.7 rebounds and 4.2 assists. His numbers did not jump through the roof and were not his most impressive, but the maturity and the unselfishness he has shown on the floor throughout the 2015-16 season were what made him special that year.

The Final Year in New York

Coming into the 2016-17 season, the New York Knicks would try to bolster the team by adding key veterans. They would make a trade to sign 2011 NBA MVP Derrick Rose, who was seemingly healthier but still trying to get back to his superstar form. They would also bring in Joakim Noah, a former Defensive Player of the Year winner, to give the team the defensive fangs they were missing since trading away Tyson Chandler. With the key additions, some were claiming that the Knicks were on their way to the playoffs, especially with a healthier and more mature Carmelo Anthony leading the way together with an improved Kristaps Porzingis.

Carmelo Anthony would open the season scoring 19 points in a blowout loss to the Cleveland Cavaliers on October 25, 2016. He would then score a then season-high 28 points on November 6 against the Utah Jazz. Melo would later outdo himself by going for 31 points six days later in a loss to the Toronto Raptors. But at that point, the Knicks were still far away from the playoff contenders everyone thought they would be. The team would lose six of their first ten games to start the regular season.

Melo would try to remedy that by leading the Knicks to three straight victories a few days later. It was on November 20 when he tied his season-high by going for 31 against the Atlanta Hawks. Five days later, he had his best performance at that point of the season by going for a new season-high of 35 points together with 13 rebounds and five assists versus the Charlotte Hornets. That was Anthony's first double-double of the season. He scored 35 again on December 6 in a win over the Heat.

On December 9 against the Sacramento Kings, Carmelo Anthony would reach an incredible personal milestone. By going for 33 points in that win, he became only one of 29 other players in league history to score 23,000 career points. He effectively became one of the 29 best scorers in the history of the NBA. But at that point, he was still on his way to score even more points. Melo also became one of only five active players at that time to have 23,000 points. The other were, LeBron James, Dirk Nowitzki, Vince Carter, and Paul Pierce, all future Hall of Famers themselves.

That season, Carmelo Anthony was more about moving up the record books considering that the Knicks were still performing not on par with other playoff teams in the East. On Christmas Day against the Boston Celtics in a win, Melo would move past Elgin Baylor as the 28th best scorer in league history after scoring 19 points. And after going for 26 points and 13 rebounds five days later in a loss to the New Orleans Pelicans, he would move past Adrian Dantley for 27th place concerning career points scored. He would then cement himself at 26 after going for 28 points in a loss to the Sixers on January 11, 2017. He moved past Robert Parish in the process.

Carmelo Anthony was not all about moving up the scoring ladder that season. He would also continue to shatter old Knicks scoring records. On January 19 in a loss to the Washington Wizards, Melo would score 25 points in the second quarter to break the previous franchise record shared by Allan Houston and Willis Reed. Both Houston and Reed scored 24 points in a single quarter for the Knicks.

Anthony would have his best scoring performance that season on January 29. In what was a quadruple-overtime game against the Atlanta Hawks, Carmelo Anthony scored a new season high of 45 points on 18 out of 36 shooting from the field. He was responsible for sending the game to overtime and second overtime by hitting the baskets that tied the game. However, he would foul out in the second overtime and would watch as his team would lose in four overtime periods.

Carmelo Anthony was not yet done climbing up the career scoring ladder. On February 12, he would have 25 points in a win against the San Antonio Spurs to move up to 25th place of the NBA's best career scorers. By doing so, he moved past Hall of Famer and former MVP Charles Barkley.

During February, Carmelo Anthony's All-Star appearance streak nearly came to an end when he was neither voted by the fans nor selected by coaches and media to take part in that year's midseason classic. However, All-Star forward Kevin Love of the Cleveland Cavaliers had to miss the game because of injury. Anthony was chosen as Love's replacement to make the All-Star Game for the 12th overall time and a 10th straight season.

As the season was nearing its final stretch, Melo and the Knicks were getting farther and farther away from contention because of critical injuries and problems with how they were running the system. Nevertheless, Melo continued to reach personal milestones. On March 12 in a loss to the Brooklyn Nets, he scored 27 points to become only one of three players in league history to collect 10,000 points for two different franchises.

In the eight seasons that Melo played for the Denver Nuggets, he had collected 13,970 points. And in his seventh season as a Knick, he reached the 10,000-point mark in that game to join only two other players in league history. Hall of Fame players Kareem Abdul-Jabbar and Elvin Hayes were the only two players to reach such a milestone before Melo did it.[xiv]

The 2016-17 regular season would end without the Knicks making the playoffs. Their leader, Carmelo Anthony, would average 22.4 points, 5.9 rebounds, and 2.9 assists. At the age of 32, Melo seemed to have already been affected by wear and tear because of how much his rebounding and assist numbers had dropped. His field goal shooting percentage also saw a low point.

While Carmelo Anthony was making a name for himself that season as one of the league's best scorers career-wise, the New York Knicks were still unable to meet expectations. Some fingers would point to how Phil Jackson's triangle offense was out of date in an NBA era where pace and space mattered most. There were also those that thought Carmelo Anthony was becoming too old and worn down to lead a rebuilding team. That was one of the reasons why he was a hot commodity in the trade rumors all season long. However, the Knicks did not have the flexibility to trade him because of the no-trade clause in Melo's contract.

Carmelo Anthony, for his part, loved being a Knick and the city of New York. However, as a basketball player, there was only so much he could do for a team that was seemingly mismanaged and hit with unfortunate setbacks such as injuries. It also was not a secret that Anthony himself could not see eye-to-eye with team management. The Knicks' struggles and Melo's frustrations with how the team was being handled all pointed out to different directions for both parties. It had already seemed like Carmelo Anthony had played his final game as a Knick back on April 12, 2017, in a win against Philadelphia.

The Trade to the Thunder

When Knicks fans thought the drama was all over when the regular season ended, it only got worse during the offseason. Before the 2017 NBA Draft, Phil Jackson announced that he was willing to involve Kristaps Porzingis, who had just finished a productive second year in the league, in trade talks believing that the organization was only doing what was necessary to make the franchise better. Some would think that it was a retaliation move on the part of Jackson, whose relationship with Porzingis also declined. But Porzingis was not the only disgruntled star.

Back in April when the season had just concluded, Phil Jackson told the media that he thought Carmelo Anthony was better off playing elsewhere considering that the Knicks were not able to make the playoffs the last four years with him as the centerpiece. Jackson also said that the team would try to explore trade options centered on Carmelo Anthony despite the difficulty of such because of the star's no-trade clause.[xv]

While pointing out that he merely wanted Carmelo Anthony to go elsewhere to shed off that "loser" label he has had the last few seasons as a Knick, circumstances would say otherwise. The relationship between the team president and franchise player had seen a decline the past season because the two could not get on the same page. Jackson was considered overly critical of how Melo held the ball too much and how he could not defend as well as the team would have wanted him to. On the other end, Anthony was not overly fond of how the Jackson stressed the triangle offense in an era that the system did not fit in anymore. This all led to the eventual meltdown of their relationship.[xvi]

Before the draft, Carmelo Anthony expressed his willingness to be traded elsewhere despite the fact that he loved New York. He had lost all trust in the management and had also lost all hope of winning a title in the Big Apple soon. This came at a time when other teams were making blockbuster deals. Melo wanted to be traded to one of the team's that have made significant roster improvements or to one that already had a stable winning environment. His top choices were the Houston Rockets, who made a trade to pair James Harden with Chris Paul, and the Cleveland Cavaliers, who have made the NBA Finals the last three seasons with LeBron James leading the way.

Because of Anthony's no-trade clause, which only he could waive, the Knicks were constrained to follow their disgruntled star's wishes. However, Melo would later retract his choice of being traded to the Cavs because of the unstable environment in Cleveland following the dismissal of their general manager and Kyrie Irving's demands to be moved elsewhere. His choice of destination, because of this, was Houston.

A three-team trade was nearly hammered down. The Knicks would have sent Anthony to Houston while taking some players from Portland. The Blazers would, in turn, receive other undesirable contracts such as Ryan Anderson's hefty price tag. However, the deal never happened because of how the Knicks changed its front office after Phil Jackson left as the president. Portland was also unsure about Ryan Anderson's enormous contract. Because a deal to Houston seemed impossible, Anthony decided to widen his list by including Cleveland again and by adding the OKC Thunder, who had just become a legitimate contender after adding Paul George to their roster to team up with reigning MVP Russell Westbrook.[xvii]

On September 23, 2017, a deal was struck between the New York Knicks and the Oklahoma City Thunder. The Knicks sent Carmelo Anthony to OKC for a package that included center Enes Kanter, shooter Doug McDermott, and a second-round draft pick for 2018.[xvii] The deal officially marked the end of Carmelo Anthony's seven-year Knicks run, which started back in 2011 when he forced the Nuggets to trade him away to a bigger market in New York.

Carmelo Anthony's run with the New York Knicks resulted in three straight playoff appearances from 2010 to 2013. The deepest they were able to reach with Anthony as their franchise star was in 2013 when the Knicks made it all the way to the second round. However, New York was never close to making the postseason the last four years when Phil Jackson took over as the president.

In the seven seasons he has played in New York, Melo amassed a total of 10,186 points and seven All-Star Game appearances. While the Knicks did not get as far as they envisioned after making the trade to get Melo back in 2011, having Anthony as their star player was the best thing to ever happen to the struggling franchise. Especially since they had not seen anything close to a semblance of success since 90's when they still had Patrick Ewing. And with Carmelo Anthony leading the New York Knicks to three of the team's four playoff appearances since 2002, the 12-time All-Star is arguably their best player since Patrick Ewing. However, the run with Anthony ended with the Knicks hoping they could rebuild around Porzingis and a new front office.

As for the Oklahoma City Thunder, they were arguably the most successful team during the offseason. They were able to acquire a two-way superstar in Paul George after giving up Victor Oladipo, who had a massive contract that did not reflect his impact or the way he played, and untested big man Domantas Sabonis. That trade with the Indiana Pacers was as lopsided as it could get considering how good of a player Paul George was for them despite the fact that the Thunder had no assurances he would stay on with the team after his contract ended a year later.

While the Paul George trade seemed lopsided, the Thunder would outdo themselves in the Carmelo Anthony deal. They gave up an offensively talented center in Enes Kanter, who could not stay on the floor too long because of his poor defensive capabilities. The other shoe-in in that trade was a three-point specialist role player in Doug McDermott. The two players combined were Carmelo Anthony, who is an excellent offensive player and a good three-point shooter but is an average defensive asset.

With Carmelo Anthony in the fold, the OKC Thunder became the league's newest super team with two other stars teaming up with triple-double machine and 2017 MVP Russell Westbrook. The Thunder gave up mediocre assets to gain two of the league's top forwards to officially shed off their status as a rebuilding team after Kevin Durant left them in 2016.

Melo was in a good situation. The Thunder were in a "win now" mode as clearly seen from the moves they pulled off during the offseason. He had also put himself in a situation he has never been in before—playing alongside two stars in their prime. Anthony has previously played with other stars. He had Allen

Iverson and Kenyon Martin back in Denver. Though AI was still putting up good numbers, he and Martin were way past their most productive years. He was then later paired with Billups, who was also an aging star at that time. And in New York, he had Amar'e Stoudemire and Tyson Chandler. But Stoudemire was often injured. Meanwhile, Chandler was getting older and was not an offensive star.

In Oklahoma City, Carmelo Anthony gets to play with two stars that are equally hungry to win championships. Russell Westbrook was just off a historical triple-double season and is still far from slowing down. Meanwhile, Paul George was also coming off his best offensive season at his prime and is a two-way star. Westbrook's presence eases off the burden on Melo to create shots for others. On the other hand, George's ability to defend at an elite level means that Anthony would not have to defend the opposing team's best small forward.[xviii]

With the increasing success of small ball in the NBA, Carmelo Anthony would be called up to start and play at the power forward position to stretch defenses and to take advantage of defensive mismatches on him. He also gives Russell Westbrook another scoring option to pass the ball to. His presence also means that defenses would not have to focus more on

Westbrook and George, who both had their best scoring seasons the past year.

However, there are also questions surrounding Carmelo Anthony's role in OKC. He was always the go-to guy. He had the ball in his hands 90% of the time. Anthony was always criticized for not passing the ball enough and for stopping offensive possessions with isolation plays. This might not work well with Westbrook, who is also a ball-dominant player. While there are no problems with Paul George's possessions because of his ability to play off the ball, the Thunder might see a problem with Anthony isolating himself to get points up on the board instead of playing within the system and off Westbrook's ability to create shots for teammates.

However, as dominant as he is when it comes to handling possessions, Melo is still a smart scorer. In an era where small ball is played at its finest, he will be charged with the duty of pulling opposing power forwards out of the paint with his ability to shoot the ball from deep. His quickness and deceptive explosiveness mean that he could also be a pick-and-roll option and a player that could tire slower defenders down with constant movement. The best part about it is that Carmelo Anthony does not need to focus on creating shots for others or defending the other team's opposing forwards. The Thunder already has

Westbrook and George to create shots for others. George, together with Andre Roberson and Steven Adams, might also be able to cover for Anthony's defensive lapses.[xviii] Melo would only need to put his energy into one aspect—scoring the ball.

Chapter 5: Team USA

Anthony has made several appearances on the USA team. Beginning in summer 2002, he was one of 12 players named to the USA Basketball Men's Junior National Team. He was a member of the bronze medal-winning Team USA. He started all five games and averaged a team-best 15.6 points per game despite playing an average of just 22.2 minutes. He was also the second-best rebounder on the team.

Anthony's next appearance was at the 2004 USA Olympic Games in Athens along with LeBron James and Dwyane Wade. He was also together with veteran players Allen Iverson, Stephon Marbury, and Tim Duncan. He played sparingly as they won the Bronze Medal that year and he averaged 2.4 points, 1.6 rebounds, and 6.8 minutes of playing time in seven of the team's eight games.

Anthony was also on the team that played in the 2008 Summer Olympics in Beijing and was again joined by James and Wade. Aptly named the "Redeem Team" to regain the gold medal for the USA after many years of settling for less, that 2008 team was a powerhouse with the likes of Kobe Bryant, Dwight Howard, Chris Bosh, and Chris Paul also on the squad, among others. The team won their games by an average margin of 32.2

points, eliminating Australia and Argentina. Although Melo would not play his best in that tournament, Anthony had his best game with 21 points against Argentina, making 3 of 14 field goals and 13 of 13 free throws. He was then instrumental in the gold medal game as the US defeated the Spanish team. Melo had 13 points in that game and averaged 11.5 points and 4.3 rebounds throughout the entire tournament.

Anthony's most recent appearance was at the 2012 Summer Olympics in London, his third straight Olympics. He joined LeBron and David Robinson as one of only three players to have played in three Olympic Games for Team USA. Anthony played in all eight games coming off the bench as the US opted to start James and Durant. He enjoyed a better Olympic tournament, averaging 16.3 points and 4.8 rebounds to help the team win their second straight Olympic gold medal against Spain once again.

On July 23, 2015, it was reported in the *New York Post* that Carmelo Anthony has informed USA Basketball and the US Olympic officials that he would attend Team USA's mini-camp on August 11-13, 2015, in Las Vegas despite the fact that he is still recovering from his February knee surgery. USAB President Jerry Colangelo had encouraged roster hopefuls to attend the camp even if they are not able to participate actively because of injuries. Anthony has not openly expressed his desire to play for the flag once again, but an appearance on the three-day mini-camp could be an expression of commitment. While Anthony has already won gold twice and bronze once for the U.S. Team, his ability to score and play all three front-court positions make him a prototype international player.

Carmelo Anthony was once again part of the U.S. Olympic Team that took part in the 2016 Rio Summer Games. Dubbed as the "Last Man Standing" from the 2008 Olympic Team that won the gold in China, Melo is set to become the only player in basketball history to win three gold medals in the Olympics. His choice of joining the team amidst the influx of younger talents is a testament to how dedicated Anthony is to his country and the game of basketball.

Chapter 6: Anthony's Personal Life

In July 2010, Anthony married long-time girlfriend, LaLa Vasquez, after a seven-year courtship. Like Anthony, Vasquez is from New York and of Puerto Rican descent. She is a television personality best known for her appearances on several reality shows including MTV's "Total Request Live" (1998-2008). The two wed at Cipriani's in New York City before 320 guests, and Michael Eric Dyson officiated the ceremony. The couple has one son, Kiyan Carmelo Anthony, who was born in March 2007. Anthony also has two brothers, Robert and Wilford, and a sister, Daphne. He has an affinity for the entertainment world and has been featured in various music videos and even a film. Anthony is also a self-proclaimed gadget geek, but his favorite hobby and pastime remains basketball.

Off the court, Anthony is well-known for his generous philanthropic efforts and ambitious business goals. In Denver, Anthony helped organize a charity Christmas party known as "A Very Melo Christmas" for less-fortunate children. In Baltimore, Anthony hosts an annual 3-on-3 tournament known as "Melo's Holding Our Own Destiny (HOOD) Movement 3-on-3 Challenge." Since joining the NBA, he has created the

Carmelo Anthony Youth Center and donated $1.5 million to the Living Classrooms Foundation, a non-profit organization that provides innovative training and community service programs for over 35,000 children, youth, and young adults in East Baltimore. The NBA scoring machine also committed $3 million for the construction of a newly designed basketball practice facility at his alma mater. According to the Syracuse's official website, Anthony's gift represents one of the largest individual donations to Syracuse University Athletics and is believed to be one of largest by a current professional athlete to their alma mater. Anthony has also received honors for donations to other charities which have exceeded $4 million dollars.

Carmelo Anthony is one of the friendliest superstars in the NBA, and he is very close friends with his Olympic teammates and draftmates LeBron James, Dwyane Wade, and Chris Bosh. His closest friend among all of the other superstars in the NBA is fellow deadly scorer Kobe Bryant, whom he had the chance to bond with back in the 2008 Beijing Olympics. The two remain close, and they even flirted with the idea of teaming up together in Los Angeles when Melo joined the free agency market.

Anthony's entrepreneurial affairs include a signature sneaker known as the Jordan Melo. He has endorsement deals that include Foot Locker, Nike, Powerade, and Sprint. Anthony produced the documentary film "Tyson," which debuted to critical acclaim at Cannes. In September 2014, Anthony, the basketball superstar, revealed his gadget geek side with the unveiling of his new venture capital firm, MELO7 Tech Partners. "I want to brand myself as the digital athlete," shares Anthony. "I really want to be a pioneer for the digital athlete, and when it comes to tech, I want to be in that space."

Chapter 7: Carmelo Anthony's Legacy and Future

The fact that Anthony has maintained a balance among family, charity, and basketball is commendable. He is a true professional who has beaten many odds to make his mark in the game. The media frenzy that follows his every move is a real testament to his impact on the game. After over a decade in the league, the interest in Anthony has only intensified. He is a respected player whom franchises want to build teams around. Anthony's moves and scoring abilities are almost unparalleled because he knows how to utilize his strength, size, and heft to create space for inside scoring.

Melo has developed into a deadly three-point sniper, especially when it is a winning situation. He is a trickster who seems to find baskets when no one else can. His astute scoring prowess is considered his best asset with his ability to take over any game on the offensive end. At more than 6'7" and 235 lbs., Anthony is recognized as a prolific scorer with a variety of smart offensive moves. He tied the record with George Gervin for most points in a single quarter at 33 in the December 2008 match against the Minnesota Timberwolves. He holds the record for most consecutive points scored in a game, 26, which he also set against the Minnesota Timberwolves in December 2010. The record for the most 3-point field goals scored in an NBA All-Star Game also belongs to Anthony, who hit eight in the 2014 game.

Additionally, Anthony is the only player in the history of the NBA to record 60+ points and 0 turnovers in a game. Moreover, Anthony is also one of only seven players in NBA history to record 60+ points and 10+ rebounds in a match. He is one of just five players to score 50+ points in multiple games for two different teams. He was the Number 2 scorer in the NBA for the 2013-2014 season and was the best in 2012-13.

Carmelo Anthony was able to pile up all of those statistics just by being a complete scorer. Ever since he came into the league in 2003, Carmelo Anthony has become one of the best scorers in the whole league and has done so in a fashion unseen from previous players. As a small forward, Melo had the handles and the shooting of a guard. He can dribble the ball smoothly out on the perimeter and then just suddenly rises for a midrange shot with a majestic shooting form that seems statuesque.

Melo is not merely a one-trick pony on offense. He is one of the best slashers in the NBA, and he can get to the basket with his dribbling skills and finish strong with his big body and athletic abilities. Aside from that, Carmelo Anthony is probably the best small forward at posting down on the low block. He has an array of post moves that put bigger men to shame. Often he just bullies his smaller defenders in the post for easy baskets. With that, Carmelo Anthony is just a pure and complete scorer.

With the Denver Nuggets, Carmelo Anthony was undoubtedly the best player and the franchise's face ever since he was drafted in 2003. He led that team in scoring for many years and failed to do so in merely one season after Allen Iverson was brought into Denver. There is also no doubt in one's mind that Carmelo Anthony is one of the best players in Denver Nuggets history. After merely playing for 7½ years with the Nuggets, Melo was already third among Denver players in many categories. He is the Nuggets' third all-time scorer at 13,970 points behind legends Alex English and Dan Issel. His total minutes and total field goals are also third behind those two players. Though Carmelo Anthony did not do enough to become the best player in Nuggets franchise history, he would have undoubtedly been such if he had chosen to stay with the team until now.

With the Knicks, Carmelo Anthony did not play long and did not do enough to belong with the likes of Patrick Ewing, Walt Frazier, Willis Reed, and Earl Monroe, among other legendary

Knicks players. However, his reputation as a pure scorer continued in when he was with the Knicks. He and Bernard King are the only Knicks players in league history ever to lead the NBA in scoring. He would also amass over 10,000 career points while playing for New York.

While Melo was not able to deliver the same team success and championships that guys like Ewing, Frazier, Reed, and Monroe have given to New York, there is no argument that Anthony is the best player the Knicks franchise has had in quite a long time. Not since the era of Patrick Ewing has a Knicks player commanded the same star power that Melo has. He would also be responsible for leading New York to three of their last four playoff appearances since 2002. And Ewing left the team in 2000, nobody in the franchise has done so much for New York than Anthony.

The list of accomplishments goes on and on for the superstar scorer because, offensively, Anthony is a beast. The numbers tell the story, and the numbers do not lie. He has carved out a place for himself in the NBA history books, stepping over the doubters and naysayers. He has excelled in the face of much adversity, rising from the streets of Baltimore, where his life could have quickly taken an alternate route, to his meteoric rise and reputation as one of the best players in the NBA.

Anthony could likely go down in history as the player who rejuvenated the fading New York franchise, which has gone more than 40 years without an NBA title. His accomplishments as a pure scorer got him mentioned in the same sentence as Jordan, Bryant, and James, and his legacy in basketball will not soon be forgotten. Still, Anthony has other plans up his tattooed sleeve.

Now as a member of a superstar-laded Oklahoma City Thunder team, Carmelo Anthony is still chasing that elusive title that has haunted him since 2003. Among the top five players drafted in 2003, he is the only one without a ring. However, he could very well end up as a champion if the stars align well for the Oklahoma City Thunder.

Nevertheless, even if he would not eventually win an NBA championship, Anthony is a diamond in the rough and already has his eyes set on a life and legacy after basketball. One thing is for sure, his time in the NBA has built the mental tenacity and character needed to be successful anywhere.

Final Word/About the Author

I was born and raised in Norwalk, Connecticut. Growing up, I could often be found spending many nights watching basketball, soccer, and football matches with my father in the family living room. I love sports and everything that sports can embody. I believe that sports are one of most genuine forms of competition, heart, and determination. I write my works to learn more about influential athletes in the hopes that from my writing, you the reader can walk away inspired to put in an equal if not greater amount of hard work and perseverance to pursue your goals. If you enjoyed *Carmelo Anthony: The Inspiring Story of One of Basketball's Most Versatile Scorers,* please leave a review! Also, you can read more of my works on *Roger Federer, Novak Djokovic, Andrew Luck, Rob Gronkowski, Brett Favre, Calvin Johnson, Drew Brees, J.J. Watt, Colin Kaepernick, Aaron Rodgers, Peyton Manning, Tom Brady, Russell Wilson, Michael Jordan, LeBron James, Kyrie Irving, Klay Thompson, Stephen Curry, Kevin Durant, Russell Westbrook, Anthony Davis, Chris Paul, Blake Griffin, Kobe Bryant, Joakim Noah, Scottie Pippen, Kevin Love, Grant Hill, Tracy McGrady, Vince Carter, Patrick Ewing, Karl Malone, Tony Parker, Allen Iverson, Hakeem Olajuwon, Reggie Miller, Michael Carter-Williams, John Wall, James Harden, Tim Duncan, Steve Nash, Draymond Green,*

Kawhi Leonard, Dwyane Wade, Ray Allen, Pau Gasol, Dirk Nowitzki, Jimmy Butler, Paul Pierce, Manu Ginobili, Pete Maravich, Larry Bird, Kyle Lowry, Jason Kidd, David Robinson, LaMarcus Aldridge, Derrick Rose, Paul George, Kevin Garnett, Chris Paul, Marc Gasol, Yao Ming, Al Horford, Amar'e Stoudemire, DeMar DeRozan, Isaiah Thomas, Kemba Walker and Chris Bosh in the Kindle Store. If you love basketball, check out my website at claytongeoffreys.com to join my exclusive list where I let you know about my latest books and give you lots of goodies.

Like what you read? Please leave a review!

I write because I love sharing the stories of influential athletes like Carmelo Anthony with fantastic readers like you. My readers inspire me to write more so please do not hesitate to let me know what you thought by leaving a review! If you love books on life, basketball, or productivity, check out my website at claytongeoffreys.com to join my exclusive list where I let you know about my latest books. Aside from being the first to hear about my latest releases, you can also download a free copy of *33 Life Lessons: Success Principles, Career Advice & Habits of Successful People*. See you there!

Clayton

References

[i] Abbott, Henry. "Carmelo Anthony in Middle School". *ESPN*. 8 February 2011. Web.

[ii] Kussoy, Howie. "Carmelo Anthony's Been Waiting His Whole Career For This Moment". *New York Post*. 12 February 2015. Web.

[iii] "Carmelo Anthony". *The Draft Review*. Web.

[iv] "Carmelo Anthony". *The Draft Review*. Web.

[v] "Carmelo Anthony". *The Draft Review*. Web.

[vi] Heller, Dave. "StaTuesday: Andrew Wiggins and 2,000 career points". *Fox Sports*. 29 December 2015. Web.

[vii] Berman, Marc. "Carmelo Anthony Craves the Allen Iverson Treatment". *New York Post*. 9 April 2016. Web.

[viii] Adande, JA. "Kobe and Melo, Friends and Foes". *ESPN*. 21 May 2009. Web.

[ix] Buckley, Zach. "Timeline of Carmelo Anthony's Journey from the Denver Nuggets to NY Knicks". *Bleacher Report*. 13 May 2013. Web.

[x] Prada, Mike. "Carmelo Anthony Press Conference: Trade to Knicks Was a 'Dream Come True'". *SBNation*. 23 Feb 2011. Web.

[xi] Abrams, Jonathan. "Anthony Makes Knicks Debut with 27 Points". *New York Times*. 23 February 2011. Web.

[xii] Shetler, Matt. "Patrick Ewing Praises Carmelo Anthony's Maturity". *Fansided*. 2012. Web.

[xiii] Weitzman, Yaron. "Carmelo Anthony is Becoming the Player Critics Always Wanted Him to Be". *SBNation*. 6 February 2016. Web.

[xiv] "Nets hold off Knicks 120-112 for 1st home win of 2017". *ESPN*. 12 March 2017. Web

[xv] Begley, Ian. "Phil Jackson: Carmelo Anthony 'better off somewhere else'". *ESPN*. 15 April 2017. Web.

[xvi] Winfield, Kristian. "Phil Jackson admits Knicks will try to trade Carmelo Anthony". *SB Nation*. 14 April 2017. Web.

[xvii] Winfield, Kristian. "Carmelo Anthony traded to Thunder in blockbuster deal". *SB Nation*. 23 September 2017. Web.

[xviii] Mahoney, Rob. "Carmelo Anthony, Paul George and the Remaking of Oklahoma City". *Sports Illustrated*. 25 September 2017. Web.

Made in the USA
Las Vegas, NV
29 November 2022